FATHERING STRONG

Fatherhood Awakening and 30-Day Devotional and Journal

BRUCE STAPLETON

For more information and resources, go to the book website at:
www.fatheringstrongbook.com

Table of Contents

Forward

When I became a father, I focused on providing stability and maintaining a consistent presence in my children's lives. I was determined to be there for every milestone - from first steps to school plays to sports games. I worked hard to ensure they had a comfortable home, nutritious meals, and access to good education. My schedule revolved around their needs, and I tried to create routines that would give them a sense of security.

But something was still missing. Despite my best efforts, I felt there was a deeper dimension to fatherhood that I hadn't yet tapped into. I was going through the motions, checking all the right boxes, but not fully understanding the profound spiritual purpose behind my role.

I only understood fatherhood's deeper purpose when I strengthened my relationship with God. Through prayer, scripture study, and fellowship with other Christian fathers, I began to see my role through a spiritual lens. I realized that being a father wasn't just about physical provision and emotional support - it was about modeling God's love, teaching eternal values, and guiding my children toward their relationship with their Heavenly Father. This spiritual awakening transformed how I parented, bringing new meaning to everyday moments and helping me parent with greater patience, wisdom, and purpose.

This book you hold in your hand (or are reading online) is your invitation to a similar transformation through a deeper connection with God. Beginning with the 7-day Fatherhood Awakening exercise, you'll experience a profound shift in how you view your role. Then, as you work through the 30-day devotional and journal, the daily reflections, Scripture readings, and journaling prompts will strengthen your faith and family relationships.

I've witnessed countless fathers discover their true identity through spiritual growth. As they connect with God's design for fatherhood, their parenting transforms. This isn't another task for your busy life—finding the spiritual center makes everything meaningful.

Remember, you're not just becoming a better father—you're allowing God to shape you into the father He designed you to be. Your commitment today will impact generations to come.

May you find abundant joy in leading your family with courage, fortitude, faith, and love flowing from profound spiritual connection. Your journey to stronger fatherhood starts here.

In His Grace,

Bruce Stapleton

Cofounder, Fathering Strong

Becoming Fathering Strong

Welcome to the Fathering Strong Fatherhood Awakening and 30-Day Devotional and Journal.

This transformative journey consists of two phases to help you become the father God designed you to be. You'll begin with the **7-Day Fatherhood Awakening**, which establishes your foundation by helping you identify your vision, strengths, and growth areas. This preparatory week then flows naturally into the **30-Day Devotional and Journal**, where you'll develop four core virtues—the courage to lead, the fortitude to persevere, the faith to trust God's guidance, and the love to nurture your family.

Together, these components create a complete process that blends biblical wisdom with practical parenting skills. You'll learn to lead with wisdom, stand firm through challenges, walk by faith, and love your children unconditionally. Throughout this journey, you'll strengthen six foundational areas essential to fatherhood: physical health to model vitality, spiritual health to guide with godly wisdom, emotional wealth to connect authentically with your children, financial stability to provide security for your family, a thriving marriage to demonstrate healthy relationships, and deep father-child bonds that foster lasting connection and trust.

Throughout this 30-day journey, you'll participate in weekly progress check-ins every seventh day. These intentional pauses allow you to evaluate your growth, celebrate victories (no matter how small), and honestly assess areas needing additional focus. Each check-in offers structured reflection questions to help you identify patterns, overcome obstacles, and adjust your approach for the coming week. This rhythm of regular assessment keeps you accountable to your goals while giving you the chance to course-correct when needed. Remember, transformation isn't about perfection—it's about consistent progress. These weekly milestones will help you maintain momentum and maximize the impact of your journal efforts each week.

To dive deeper into the four core pillars and six foundational strengths of fatherhood, visit www.fatheringstrongbook.com. This devotional partners with the book "Fathering Strong - God's Blueprint for Leading Your Family," which provides real fatherhood stories and biblical wisdom for each virtue and core strength. You'll find free downloadable templates, additional resources, and practical tools to support your journey. Consider purchasing a copy to maximize the impact of your 30-day journey and access to the complete fatherhood blueprint.

Remember, meaningful change happens through small, consistent steps taken with purpose and prayer. As you begin this journey, commit to showing up each day with an open heart and willing spirit. Your investment in becoming a stronger father will impact your children and future generations.

Let's start this exciting journey together.

Part 1: The 7-Day Fatherhood Awakening

As fathers, we often jump straight into action. When we see a problem, our instinct is to fix it immediately. But what if taking a step back—spending just one week in thoughtful reflection—could dramatically improve our effectiveness as fathers for years to come?

Why Preparation Matters

The 30-day Fathering Strong Devotional and Journal offers powerful tools to transform your fatherhood journey. But without proper preparation, you risk missing its full impact. Think of it like building a house: no matter how excellent your materials and tools are, you're just hammering boards together and hoping for the best without a blueprint.

The 7-Day Fatherhood Awakening serves as your blueprint creation process. It helps you:

> ➤ Identify which areas of fatherhood need your immediate attention

> ➤ Understand the underlying values that will guide your decisions

> ➤ Create specific, achievable goals rather than vague aspirations

> ➤ Prioritize your efforts where they'll make the greatest difference

The Six Foundational Strengths × Four Core Virtues Framework

What makes this 7-day Fatherhood Awakening process uniquely powerful is its comprehensive framework. Rather than focusing on just one aspect of fatherhood, it examines six foundational strengths:

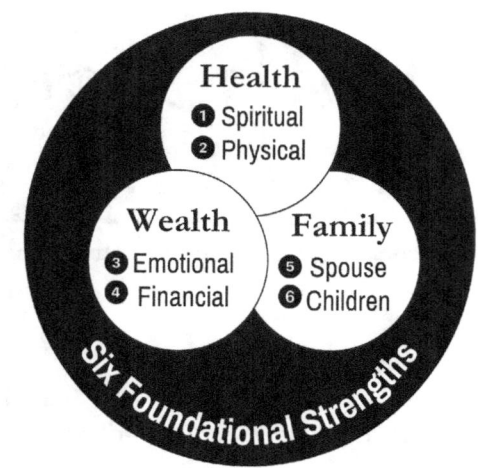

1. **Physical Health** - The energy and vitality to be present for your family

2. **Spiritual Health** - The foundation of your moral leadership

3. **Emotional Wealth** - Your capacity for connection and resilience

4. **Financial Wealth** - Your ability to provide and create opportunity

5. **Marriage Relationships** - The cornerstone of family stability

6. **Child Connections** - The heart of your fathering legacy

These six areas are then examined through the lens of four timeless core virtues:

1. **Courage** - Facing brutal truths and taking bold action

2. **Fortitude** - Persevering through challenges with determination

3. **Faith** - Trusting in something greater than yourself

4. **Love** - Expressing selfless care and commitment

This creates a powerful 24-point matrix that ensures no critical aspect of fatherhood goes unexamined. When a father honestly evaluates himself across all these dimensions, patterns emerge, revealing both strengths to leverage and weaknesses to address.

While this framework may sound complex, I have designed the process to be straightforward and accessible. You won't be left wondering what to do or how to proceed. Each day includes simple templates and guided questions that make self-reflection effortless. For example, you'll rate yourself on specific questions for each strength area and virtue combination during your self-assessment.

For instance, one of the questions asks: "On a scale of 1-10, how effectively do you feel you're taking action to improve your health despite facing obstacles?"

These ratings quickly reveal patterns, showing you where to focus your energy: no guesswork, no confusion—just clarity. The assessment takes minutes, but the insights will transform your approach to fatherhood. I've removed all barriers to make this process as simple as possible while maintaining the depth needed for meaningful change.

The Divine Pattern: Six Days of Work, One Day of Rest

The structure of this Fatherhood Awakening follows the divine pattern established at creation: six days of purposeful work followed by a day of rest and reflection. This is no coincidence. Just as God demonstrated the perfect balance of action and reflection, your fatherhood journey requires both focused effort and thoughtful review.

Days 1-6 will stretch you, challenge you, and possibly uncover uncomfortable truths. The seventh day provides the space to integrate these insights into a cohesive blueprint that will guide your next 30 days and beyond.

Need a boost of motivation and daily reminders? You're welcome to enroll in the online version of the 7-day Fatherhood Awakening. You'll receive daily emails, including forms you can complete online and print out. If that's more your style, simply visit *www.fatheringstrongbook.com* to enroll in the online version of the 7-day Fatherhood Awakening program.

The Day-by-Day Journey Snapshot

Day 1: Finding Your "Why"

Everything begins with purpose. Even the best tactics will eventually falter without a compelling vision for your fatherhood. Day 1 helps you articulate your deepest aspirations as a father, creating a north star that will guide all your future decisions. "Where there is no vision, the people perish" (Proverbs 29:18).

Day 2: Honest Self-Assessment

Growth requires truth. Day 2 guides you through a comprehensive self-evaluation across all six strength areas and four virtues. This isn't about shame or comparison—it's about establishing a clear starting point for your journey. "Search me, O God, and know my heart; test me and know my anxious thoughts" (Psalm 139:23).

Days 3-5: Deep Dive Into Foundational Fatherhood Strengths

These three days help you understand how each virtue manifests in different areas of your life:

> ➤ Day 3 focuses on your foundational health (physical and spiritual) - "Do you not know that your bodies are temples of the Holy Spirit?" (1 Corinthians 6:19)

> ➤ Day 4 examines your wealth-building (emotional and financial) - "For where your treasure is, there your heart will be also" (Matthew 6:21)

> ➤ Day 5 explores your family relationships (marriage and children) - "Husbands, love your wives, just as Christ loved the church" (Ephesians 5:25)

Day 6: Setting SMART Goals and Priorities

With clear understanding comes focused action. Day 6 helps you translate insights into specific, measurable goals and prioritize them for maximum impact. "Commit to the Lord whatever you do, and he will establish your plans" (Proverbs 16:3).

Day 7: Finalizing Your Blueprint

The culmination of your week's work is a comprehensive blueprint that integrates your vision, assessment results, and prioritized goals into a cohesive guide for your 30-day journey. "For which of you, desiring to build a tower, does not first sit down and count the cost?" (Luke 14:28).

The Cost of Skipping This Process

Some fathers, eager to begin their journey, might be tempted to bypass this preparation week. Yet Scripture reminds us of the wisdom in careful planning: "The plans of the diligent lead surely to abundance, but everyone who is hasty comes only to poverty" (Proverbs 21:5).

Consider what you'd be missing:

> ➤ **Clarity:** As Psalm 119:105 reminds us, "Your word is a lamp to my feet and a light to my path." How will you recognize the path forward without knowing where you stand today?

- ➤ **Focus**: Jesus taught us in Matthew 6:24 that "No one can serve two masters." With limited time and energy, shouldn't you discern where God calls you to invest?

- ➤ **Motivation**: "Let us not grow weary of doing good, for in due season we will reap if we do not give up" (Galatians 6:9). When challenges arise, a God-inspired vision sustains you.

- ➤ **Accountability**: "But be doers of the word, and not hearers only, deceiving yourselves" (James 1:22). Specific goals create the framework for faithful action.

One week of prayerful preparation now will multiply the effectiveness of the month that follows. It's the difference between building your house on sand or on the rock (Matthew 7:24-27).

Your Journey Begins With a Single Step

The father you want to become—the father your family deserves—is waiting on the other side of these seven days. The reflection challenge isn't just about filling out worksheets or answering questions; it's about intentionally designing the blueprint for your fatherhood legacy.

As you begin this process, remember that honest self-reflection requires courage. Setting meaningful priorities demands fortitude. Trusting the process calls for faith. And your commitment to growth demonstrates love for your family in its purest form.

Your seven-day investment now will yield returns for generations to come. Are you ready to begin?

7-Day Fatherhood Awakening

Understand Your Why — Day 1

Day 2 — **Fatherhood Self-assessment**

Health Foundational Strengths — Day 3

Day 3 - 5 Foundational Strength Deep Dive

Day 4 — **Wealth Foundational Strengths**

Family Foundational Strengths — Day 5

Day 6 — **Goal Setting and Priorities**

Rest and Reflect — Day 7

Day 1: Your Fathering Strong Vision Statement

Creating a clear vision for your fatherhood journey is the first step before setting specific goals. This vision serves as your North Star, providing direction and purpose to guide all your parenting decisions and actions. Just as a builder needs blueprints before construction, a father needs a well-defined vision before developing SMART goals and action plans. This vision will help you focus on what truly matters, deepen your connection with your children, and transform your aspirations into reality. Use this worksheet to reflect deeply on your values, define your purpose, and craft a compelling vision to guide you toward becoming a Fathering Strong dad.

Create your Fathering Strong Vision in three easy steps.

Below is a simple but powerful process to develop your fatherhood vision. By working through these three steps, you'll gain clarity about the father you want to be:

1. **Reflect on Your Role as a Father** - Discover your deeper purpose and meaning in fatherhood

2. **Identify Your Core Values** - Determine what principles will guide your parenting decisions

3. **Reflect on your experiences with your father** - Look at both the positive and negative experiences

Take your time with each step. The insights you gain will form the foundation of your fathering journey and help you create your Fathering Strong vision statement—one that will profoundly impact your future and your family.

Step 1: Reflect on Your Role as a Father

What does being a father mean to you on a deeper level? Consider your purpose beyond daily responsibilities like providing and protecting. Are you a guide, a teacher, a role model, a nurturer, or a combination of these? Reflect on attributes like:

➤ Emotional anchor – providing stability and security

➤ Moral compass – teaching right from wrong

➤ Life coach – helping navigate challenges

➤ Memory maker – creating meaningful experiences

➤ Identity shaper – helping form their sense of self

➤ Legacy builder – passing down values and traditions

Think about times when you felt most fulfilled as a father. What were you doing? How were you connecting? These insights often reveal your deeper purpose.

Here are a few resource suggestions to help you reflect:

➢ **Childhood Memories:** Reflect on positive memories from your childhood. What did your father or other role models do that made you feel valued and loved?

➢ **Feedback from Others:** Ask your spouse, co-parent, or trusted friends what they observe about your parenting strengths. Sometimes, others see qualities in us that we don't recognize.

➢ **YouTube videos**: Here are four excellent videos to spark your thoughts about fatherhood and what this journey means to you.

  o 5 Minutes for the Next 50 Years - Crafting Your Own Identity: Insights from Matthew McConaughey
  (https://www.youtube.com/watch?v=QbL0X3B4mjg)

  o Think About Your Family- Eric Thomas is a fantastic speaker. In this classic motivational speech, he empowers us to believe that we can always overcome adversity, no matter the challenge.
  (https://www.youtube.com/watch?v=Js6SOhWm9a4)

  o Tony Dungy's Emotional Speech About Being a Dad - Super Bowl Winning NFL Head Coach Tony Dungy shares the most important lesson he has ever learned about being a father.
  (https://www.youtube.com/watch?v=MaE-5_J9m-E)

  o What Every Son Needs From His Father - Tierce Green presents five essential things for a healthy father and son relationship. This video specifically focuses on fathers and sons, but the principles also apply to fathers and daughters.
  (https://www.youtube.com/watch?v=5Q1g1Yt-urQ)

➢ **Fatherhood Community**: Connect with other fathers you know, share experiences, and gain new perspectives on your fathering journey.

List your top 3 things that fatherhood means to you.

1.

2.

3.

What kind of father do you want your children to see? Consider the qualities you demonstrate that you hope your children will naturally embrace. List the top 3 qualities.

1.

2.

3.

Now, take what you have listed and see if you can come up with the three words that best describe the father you aspire to be.

1.

2.

3.

Step 2: Identify Your Core Values

Core values are the foundational beliefs and principles that guide your decisions and actions as a father. They represent what you believe is most important in life and parenting. These values serve as your internal compass, helping you navigate difficult situations and make consistent choices that align with who you want to be as a father.

Why core values matter for fathers:

> ➢ They provide consistency in your parenting approach

> ➢ They help you make difficult decisions with clarity

> ➢ They show your children what matters most through your example

> ➢ They create a foundation for your family culture

How to Identify Your Core Values:

> ➢ Reflect on moments when you felt most proud as a father. What values were you expressing in those moments?

> ➢ Consider what you want your children to remember about you. The qualities you hope they'll mention when describing you to others often reflect your core values.

> ➢ Think about what makes you feel fulfilled and purposeful in your role as a father. These feelings often connect to your deepest values.

> ➢ Examine your reactions to challenging situations. What principles do you find yourself defending or prioritizing when under pressure?

Examples of Core Values for Fathers:

> ➢ **Integrity:** Being honest and consistent in words and actions

> ➢ **Presence:** Being fully engaged and available for your children

> ➢ **Compassion:** Showing empathy and kindness toward your children's struggles

> ➢ **Responsibility:** Being accountable for your actions and teaching children to do the same

> ➢ **Growth:** Encouraging continuous learning and improvement

> ➢ **Faith:** Nurturing spiritual development and religious practices

> ➢ **Resilience:** Teaching children to persevere through challenges

> ➢ **Respect:** Treating others with dignity and consideration

> ➢ **Service:** Contributing positively to family and community

> ➢ **Joy:** Celebrating life and finding happiness in everyday moments

Remember that your core values should be authentic to you. They should reflect who you truly are and who you aspire to be as a father, not what others expect of you.

Biblical Guidance for Fatherhood Values

Scripture offers profound wisdom for fathers seeking to establish their core values. Consider these passages as you reflect on your role:

> ➢ **Deuteronomy 6:6-7** - "These commandments that I give you today are to be on your hearts. Impress them on your children. Talk about them when you sit at home and when you walk along the road, when you lie down, and when you get up." This emphasizes the importance of consistently teaching values through everyday moments.

> ➢ **Ephesians 6:4** - "Fathers, do not exasperate your children; instead, bring them up in the training and instruction of the Lord." This reminds us to balance discipline with nurturing guidance.

> ➢ **Proverbs 22:6** - "Start children off on the way they should go, and even when they are old, they will not turn from it." This highlights the lasting impact of early value formation.

> ➢ **Psalm 103:13** - "As a father has compassion on his children, so the Lord has compassion on those who fear him." This models the compassionate heart of fatherhood.

> ➢ **Joshua 24:15** - "But as for me and my household, we will serve the Lord." This demonstrates the power of making clear value declarations for your family.

As you identify your core values, consider how these biblical principles might inform and strengthen your vision for fatherhood.

What key values do you want to pass on to your children? (e.g., kindness, honesty, responsibility, faith). List your top 3:

1.

2.

3.

How will you demonstrate these values in your daily life? Identify one way for each of the 3 values you identified.

1.

2.

3.

Step 3: Your Experience with Your Father

How did your experiences with your father (or father figures) shape who you want to be as a father?

Consider both the positive lessons and the gaps in your upbringing. Add your top 3 positives and top 3 negatives; if you don't have that many in either category, list as many (or any) as you remember.

If you grew up without a father or father figure, consider looking to other positive male role models you've encountered—perhaps uncles, teachers, coaches, or mentors. You can also reflect on what you wished for but didn't receive, using these insights to shape the father you want to become. Sometimes, our strongest parenting values emerge from recognizing what was missing in our childhood.

Reflecting on your relationship with your father or father figure can provide powerful insights into the kind of father you want to be. Take some time to consider meaningful moments that shaped you.

For positive experiences, think about:

➢ Times when your father made you feel valued, seen, or understood

➢ Traditions or activities you enjoyed together (sports games, fishing trips, reading together)

➢ How he showed up during important milestones or difficult moments

➢ Specific words of wisdom or encouragement that stayed with you

➢ Ways he demonstrated his values through actions

For negative experiences, consider:

➢ Moments when you felt unsupported, criticized, or misunderstood

➢ Patterns of behavior that created distance or hurt

➢ Important events where he was absent (physically or emotionally)

➢ Values or behaviors you've consciously decided not to repeat

➢ Needs that went unmet in your relationship

Remember, this reflection isn't about judging your father but understanding how these experiences influence your fatherhood journey. Even difficult experiences can provide valuable lessons about the father you want to become.

List your positive and negative experiences:

Positive experiences:

1.

2.

3.

Negative experiences:

1.

2.

3.

Based on these experiences and reflections, what three things do you want your children to feel from their relationship with you as their father?

1.

2.

3.

Complete Your Vision Statement as a Father

Congratulations! You've completed the hard work of reflection and self-discovery. Now, it's time to bring everything together into your personal fatherhood vision statement. This statement will serve as your guiding light and daily inspiration. Below is a template to help you organize your thoughts, but feel free to craft your vision in a way that feels authentic and meaningful to you.

As a father, I strive to be _____, _____, and _____ (three aspirational qualities) for my children.

Through my actions, I will demonstrate the values of _____, _____, and _____ (your core values)

by _____
(specific ways you'll show these values).

Drawing from my experiences, I will build upon the positive aspects of

_____ (positive experiences)

while consciously avoiding _____ (negative experiences).

My ultimate goal is to create a home where my children feel _____, _____, and _____
(desired environment/feelings for your children)

while helping them develop into _____
(the type of people you hope they become).

Example Vision Statements Using Template:

"As a father, I strive to be patient, present, and nurturing for my children. Through my actions, I will demonstrate the values of integrity, compassion, and perseverance by modeling these behaviors in daily life and discussing their importance. Drawing from my experiences, I will build upon the positive aspects of family traditions and quality time while consciously avoiding criticism and emotional distance. My ultimate goal is to create a home where my children feel loved, secure, and empowered while helping them develop into confident, empathetic individuals who pursue their passions."

"As a father, I strive to be consistent, encouraging, and wise for my children. Through my actions, I will demonstrate the values of honesty, responsibility, and kindness by teaching through example and celebrating their efforts. Drawing from my experiences, I will build upon the positive aspects of open communication and unconditional support while consciously avoiding harsh judgment and unrealistic expectations. My ultimate goal is to create a home where my children feel accepted, inspired, and understood while helping them develop into resilient, compassionate leaders."

"As a father, I strive to be supportive, authentic, and dependable for my children. Through my actions, I will demonstrate the values of respect, curiosity, and determination by actively engaging in their interests and showing genuine care. Drawing from my experiences, I will build upon the positive aspects of shared adventures and meaningful conversations while consciously avoiding emotional unavailability and inconsistency. My ultimate goal is to create a home where my children feel valued, safe, and confident while helping them develop into independent, well-rounded individuals who positively contribute to their community."

For a printable copy of the Fathering Strong 30-day Daily Devotional and Journal Vision worksheet and other online resources, go to *www.fatheringstrongbook.com.*

Day 2: Fatherhood Self-Assessment

Introduction

Welcome to Day 2 of the **Fatherhood Awakening Process**. Yesterday, you created a vision of the father you aspire to be. Today, we'll conduct an honest self-assessment to identify your current strengths and areas for growth. Proverbs 27:19 reminds us, "As water reflects the face, so one's life reflects the heart." This assessment will help you reflect on your heart and life as a father.

Purpose of Self-Assessment

Self-awareness is the foundation of meaningful growth. As we read in 2 Corinthians 13:5, "Examine yourselves to see whether you are in the faith; test yourselves." This assessment will help you understand where you currently stand in relation to your fatherhood vision, allowing you to set focused, meaningful goals later in this process.

Assessment Framework

The assessment examines the intersection of four core virtues with six foundational strengths:

Core Virtues

1. **Courage** - The strength to do what is right regardless of fear or opposition (Joshua 1:9)

2. **Fortitude** - The resilience and determination to persevere through challenges (James 1:12)

3. **Faith** - Trust and confidence in God and His promises (Hebrews 11:1)

4. **Love** - Selfless commitment to the good of others (1 Corinthians 13:4-7)

Foundational Strengths

1. **Physical Health** - Your bodily well-being and vitality

2. **Spiritual Health** - Your relationship with God and spiritual growth

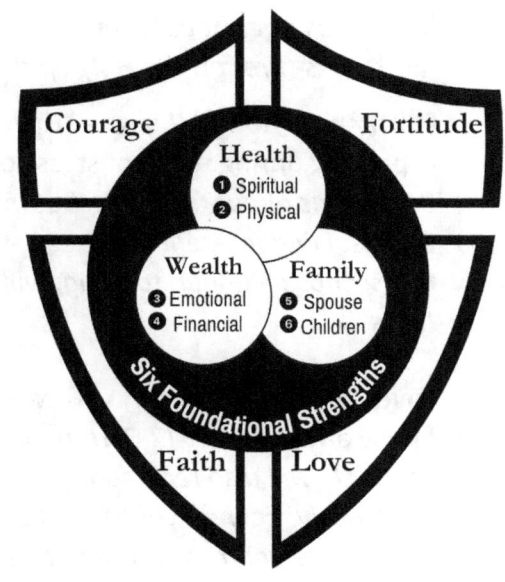

3. **Emotional Wealth** - Your emotional intelligence and stability

4. **Financial Wealth** - Your stewardship of resources and provision

5. **Marriage Relationship** - Your connection with your spouse

6. **Connections with Children** - Your bonds with your children

The Assessment Process

You'll evaluate yourself on 24 questions (one for each intersection of virtue and strength) on a scale of 1-10:

➤ 1-3: Significant opportunity for growth

➤ 4-6: Developing but inconsistent

➤ 7-8: Consistent strength

➤ 9-10: Exemplary strength

Sample Assessment Questions

Courage × Physical Health - "How willing am I to make difficult choices regarding my physical wellbeing, even when uncomfortable?" *(1 Corinthians 6:19-20 – "Do you not know that your bodies are temples of the Holy Spirit, who is in you, whom you have received from God? You are not your own; you were bought at a price. Therefore, honor God with your bodies.")*

Fortitude × Spiritual Health - "How consistently do I maintain spiritual disciplines even during busy or challenging seasons?" *(Romans 5:3-5 - "Not only so, but we[a] also glory in our sufferings, because we know that suffering produces perseverance; perseverance, character; and character, hope. And hope does not put us to shame because God's love has been poured out into our hearts through the Holy Spirit, who has been given to us.")*

Faith × Emotional Wealth - "How much do I trust God with my emotions, especially during times of stress or uncertainty?" *(Philippians 4:6-7 – "Do not be anxious about anything, but in every situation, by prayer and petition, with thanksgiving, present your requests to God. And the peace of God, which transcends all understanding, will guard your hearts and your minds in Christ Jesus.")*

Love × Financial Wealth - "How generously do I use my resources to bless my family and others?" *(2 Corinthians 9:6-8 - Remember this: Whoever sows sparingly will also reap sparingly, and whoever sows generously will also reap generously. Each of you should give what you have decided in your heart to give, not reluctantly or under compulsion, for God loves a cheerful giver. And*

God is able to bless you abundantly, so that in all things at all times, having all that you need, you will abound in every good work.")

Courage × Marriage Relationship - "How willing am I to have difficult conversations with my spouse to strengthen our relationship?" *(Ephesians 4:15 - Instead, speaking the truth in love, we will grow to become in every respect the mature body of him who is the head, that is, Christ.")*

Fortitude × Connections with Children - "How persistent am I in engaging with my children even when tired or distracted?" *(Deuteronomy 6:6-7 - These commandments that I give you today are to be on your hearts. Impress them on your children. Talk about them when you sit at home and when you walk along the road, when you lie down and when you get up.")*

Scoring and Interpretation

After completing all 24 questions:

1. Calculate your total score for each core virtue (add scores across the six foundational strengths)

2. Calculate your total score for each foundational strength (add scores across the four core virtues)

3. Identify your highest and lowest-scoring areas

Your lowest scores indicate priority areas for growth. However, remember what Paul writes in Philippians 3:12-14 about pressing forward toward the goal. This assessment isn't about judgment but about identifying your starting point for growth.

Reflection Questions

After completing the assessment, consider:

➢ What patterns do you notice in your scores?

➢ Which virtue seems most challenging for you to embody as a father?

➢ Which area of your life seems to need the most attention?

➢ What surprised you about your assessment results?

➢ How do your results compare to the vision you created on Day 1?

Next Steps

Tomorrow, we'll begin exploring how each core virtue connects with the foundational strengths, starting with health-related foundational strengths of physical and spiritual health. This deeper understanding will help you develop specific, actionable goals to strengthen your role as a father.

Remember, *"He who began a good work in you will carry it on to completion until the day of Christ Jesus" (Philippians 1:6).* **This assessment is not about perfection but progress on your fatherhood journey.**

Fatherhood Awakening Self-Evaluation Process

Instructions

Rate yourself on a scale of 1-10 for each question:

- ➢ 1-3: Significant opportunity for growth
- ➢ 4-6: Developing but inconsistent
- ➢ 7-8: Consistent strength
- ➢ 9-10: Exemplary strength

Be completely honest with yourself. As Psalm 139:23-24 reminds us: "Search me, God, and know my heart; test me and know my anxious thoughts. See if there is any offensive way in me, and lead me in the way everlasting."

You may take the evaluation on the proceeding pages or go to www.fatheringstrongbook.com to take the assessment online.

COURAGE

"Be strong and courageous. Do not be afraid; do not be discouraged, for the LORD your God will be with you wherever you go." (Joshua 1:9)

Courage × Physical Health

1. How willing am I to make difficult choices regarding my physical well-being, even when uncomfortable?

Score (1-10): _____

Courage × Spiritual Health

2. How boldly do I stand for my faith and values, even when facing opposition or ridicule?

Score (1-10): _____

Courage × Emotional Wealth

3. How willing am I to acknowledge and address my emotional weaknesses and blind spots?

Score (1-10): _____

Courage × Financial Wealth

4. How willing am I to make difficult financial decisions that prioritize long-term family welfare over short-term comfort?

Score (1-10): _____

Courage × Marriage Relationship

5. How willing am I to have difficult conversations with my spouse to strengthen our relationship?

Score (1-10): _____

Courage × Connections with Children

6. How willing am I to enforce necessary boundaries and discipline, even when it's difficult?

Score (1-10): _____

COURAGE TOTAL: _____

FORTITUDE

"Blessed is the one who perseveres under trial because, having stood the test, that person will receive the crown of life that the Lord has promised to those who love him." (James 1:12)

Fortitude × Physical Health

7. How consistently do I maintain healthy habits even when busy, stressed, or tired?

Score (1-10): _____

Fortitude × Spiritual Health

8. How consistently do I maintain spiritual discipline even during busy or challenging seasons?

Score (1-10): _____

Fortitude × Emotional Wealth

9. How well do I maintain emotional stability during stressful or challenging situations?

Score (1-10): _____

Fortitude × Financial Wealth

10. How disciplined am I in maintaining financial responsibility, even when faced with temptations?

Score (1-10): _____

Fortitude × Marriage Relationship

11. How persistently do I work to improve my marriage, even during difficult seasons?

Score (1-10): _____

Fortitude × Connections with Children

12. How persistent am I in engaging with my children, even when tired or distracted?

Score (1-10): _____

FORTITUDE TOTAL: _____

FAITH

"Now faith is confidence in what we hope for and assurance about what we do not see." (Hebrews 11:1)

Faith × Physical Health

13. How much do I trust God with my physical well-being, acknowledging both my responsibility and His sovereignty?

Score (1-10): _____

Faith × Spiritual Health

14. How deeply do I trust God's Word and apply it to my daily life and decisions?

Score (1-10): _____

Faith × Emotional Wealth

15. How much do I trust God with my emotions, especially during times of stress or uncertainty?

Score (1-10): _____

Faith × Financial Wealth

16. How much do I trust God's provision and principles in my financial decisions?

Score (1-10): _____

Faith × Marriage Relationship

17. How much do I trust God's design for marriage and follow biblical principles in relating to my spouse?

Score (1-10): _____

Faith × Connections with Children

18. How much do I trust God's promises for my children and His guidance in raising them?

Score (1-10): _____

FAITH TOTAL: _____

LOVE

"Love is patient, love is kind. It does not envy, it does not boast, it is not proud. It does not dishonor others, it is not self-seeking, it is not easily angered, it keeps no record of wrongs." (1 Corinthians 13:4-5)

Love × Physical Health

19. How well do I care for my physical health as an act of love toward my family?

Score (1-10): _____

Love × Spiritual Health

20. How consistently do I demonstrate God's love through my spiritual example and leadership?

Score (1-10): _____

Love × Emotional Wealth

21. How well do I express appropriate emotions and create a loving emotional atmosphere at home?

Score (1-10): _____

Love × Financial Wealth

22. How generously do I use my resources to bless my family and others?

Score (1-10): _____

Love × Marriage Relationship

23. How well do I demonstrate sacrificial love and affection toward my spouse?

Score (1-10): _____

Love × Connections with Children

24. How well do I demonstrate unconditional love to my children through both words and actions?

Score (1-10): _____

LOVE TOTAL: _____

FOUNDATIONAL STRENGTHS TOTALS

Physical Health Total (Questions 1, 7, 13, 19): _____

Spiritual Health Total (Questions 2, 8, 14, 20): _____

Emotional Wealth Total (Questions 3, 9, 15, 21): _____

Financial Wealth Total (Questions 4, 10, 16, 22): _____

Marriage Relationship Total (Questions 5, 11, 17, 23): _____

Connections with Children Total (Questions 6, 12, 18, 24): _____

REFLECTION

After completing this assessment:

> ➤ Circle your two lowest Core Virtue totals.
>
> ➤ Circle your two lowest Foundational Strength totals.
>
> ➤ Review the intersections of these areas—these may be priority growth areas.

Remember, "Being confident of this, that he who began a good work in you will carry it on to completion until the day of Christ Jesus." (Philippians 1:6)

This assessment isn't about condemnation but about identifying starting points for growth in your fatherhood journey.

Day 3: Health Foundation – Physical and Spiritual

The Fatherhood Awakening Process: Days 1-3

In Days 1-2 of your Fatherhood Awakening journey, you laid the essential groundwork by creating your personal fatherhood vision and completing a thorough self-assessment. You identified which of the four core virtues (courage, fortitude, faith, and love) and six foundational strengths require your focused attention for growth.

As you enter Day 3, you'll explore your foundational strengths more deeply, starting with the health foundation. Today focuses on your physical and spiritual health—two critical pillars supporting everything else in your fatherhood journey. You'll identify specific areas needing improvement through targeted reflection questions based on the core virtues.

This reflective work prepares you for Day 6, where you'll transform these insights into SMART goals designed to create meaningful, lasting change in your role as a father. Let's begin examining how health impacts your fatherhood's effectiveness.

Physical Health

Physical Health forms the bedrock of your ability to serve and lead your family effectively. When you prioritize your physical well-being, you model self-care and discipline for your children while ensuring you have the energy to meet your family's needs. Scripture reminds us that "your body is a temple of the Holy Spirit" (1 Corinthians 6:19-20), calling us to honor God with our physical choices.

As fathers, our physical condition directly impacts our capacity to engage, protect, and provide. Consider how your energy levels, strength, and overall health affect your patience, presence, and ability to participate fully in family activities.

Assessment Areas:

➢ Sleep patterns: Are you getting 7-8 hours of quality sleep? Poor sleep affects decision-making and emotional regulation.

➢ Nutrition: Does your diet fuel your body appropriately? "Whether you eat or drink or whatever you do, do it all for the glory of God" (1 Corinthians 10:31).

➢ Exercise routine: Regular physical activity improves mood, energy, and longevity.

> Preventative care: When was your last physical? Are you modeling responsible healthcare?

Reflection Questions:

> Courage: "What health changes have I been avoiding out of fear or discomfort?"

> Fortitude: "How can I maintain healthy habits even during busy or stressful seasons?"

> Faith: "How does viewing my body as God's temple change my health decisions?"

> Love: "What specific health goals would help me better serve my family?"

Spiritual Health

Spiritual Health anchors your family's moral compass and provides the foundation for meaningful relationships and purposeful living. Your spiritual leadership sets the tone for your family's faith journey as Joshua declared, "As for me and my household, we will serve the LORD" (Joshua 24:15).

A father's spiritual vitality influences his decision-making, values transmission, and ability to guide his family through life's challenges with wisdom and grace.

Assessment Areas:

> Prayer life: Are you consistently communicating with God? "Pray without ceasing" (1 Thessalonians 5:17).

> Scripture engagement: How regularly are you in God's Word? "Your word is a lamp for my feet, a light on my path" (Psalm 119:105).

> Community connection: Are you actively involved in a faith community that supports your growth?

> Spiritual leadership practices: How are you intentionally leading your family spiritually? "Fathers, do not exasperate your children; instead, bring them up in the training and instruction of the Lord" (Ephesians 6:4).

Reflection Questions:

> Courage: "Where do I need to step up as a spiritual leader in my home?"

> Fortitude: "What spiritual disciplines am I committed to maintaining daily?"

- ➤ Faith: "How can I better trust God's guidance in my family's challenges?"

- ➤ Love: "What practical ways can I demonstrate Christ's love to my family?"

Self-Reflection Integration: Identifying Your Growth Priorities

As you complete your health foundation assessment, it's time to synthesize your insights and identify your highest-leverage growth opportunities. This critical step transforms reflection into action by focusing your efforts where they'll create the most significant impact on your fatherhood journey.

Priority Selection Process

For each foundational strength area (beginning with physical and spiritual health), select 2-3 specific aspects that:

- ➤ Have the most significant impact on your effectiveness as a father

- ➤ Align with your personal fatherhood vision

- ➤ Currently present the most significant gap between your current state and your desired state

- ➤ Would create positive ripple effects across multiple areas of your fatherhood

Remember: Effective growth comes not from trying to improve everything simultaneously but from focused effort on your most significant opportunities. As you identify these priorities, consider which core virtue (courage, fortitude, faith, or love) you must emphasize to progress in each area.

Priority Documentation Template

For each foundational strength, complete the following:

Physical Health Priorities

Priority:

Current reality:

Desired state:

Core virtue needed:

Priority:

Current reality:

Desired state:

Core virtue needed:

Priority:

Current reality:

Desired state:

Core virtue needed:

Spiritual Health Priorities

Priority:

Current reality:

Desired state:

Core virtue needed:

Priority:

Current reality:

Desired state:

Core virtue needed:

Priority:

Current reality:

Desired state:

Core virtue needed:

As you complete this process for each foundational strength in the coming days, you'll develop a comprehensive map of your highest-impact growth opportunities. This focused approach ensures you invest your limited time and energy where it matters most for your family.

Moving Forward in Your Fatherhood Journey

As you complete today's foundational health assessment, remember that this process is not about perfection but progress. Each small step toward growth in your physical and spiritual health will yield dividends in your fatherhood effectiveness. Tomorrow, on Day 4, we'll continue building on this foundation by examining your emotional and financial wealth —equally vital components of your fatherhood blueprint.

Before closing today's work, take a moment to pray over the priorities you've identified. Ask for wisdom as James 1:5 instructs: "If any of you lacks wisdom, you should ask God, who gives generously to all without finding fault, and it will be given to you." Allow this Scripture to guide your reflection tonight, inviting God's perspective on your growth areas and seeking His strength for the journey ahead. Your commitment to this process is a powerful testament to your love for your family and your desire to lead them well.

Notes

Day 4: Wealth Foundation - Emotional and Financial Wealth

As you enter Day 4 of your Fatherhood Awakening journey, we shift our focus to the Wealth Foundation—specifically your emotional and financial wealth. These two foundational strengths profoundly impact your ability to lead your family with stability and wisdom. Today's reflections will help you identify key growth areas in managing both your emotional resources and financial stewardship.

Emotional Wealth

Emotional Wealth encompasses your ability to understand, process, and express emotions in healthy ways. As a father, your emotional intelligence directly impacts your family relationships, particularly how your children learn to navigate their emotions. Scripture reminds us to "be quick to listen, slow to speak and slow to become angry" (James 1:19), emphasizing the importance of emotional self-regulation.

Your emotional wealth determines how you respond to stress, conflict, and daily challenges. Children learn emotional regulation primarily through observation, making your example their most powerful teacher.

Assessment Areas:

➢ Self-awareness: Can you accurately identify your emotions and understand their triggers?

➢ Emotional regulation: How effectively do you manage strong emotions, especially during family conflicts?

➢ Stress management: What healthy coping mechanisms have you developed for life's pressures?

➢ Emotional availability: Are you present and attuned to your family's emotional needs? "Fathers, do not embitter your children, or they will become discouraged" (Colossians 3:21).

Reflection Questions:

➢ Courage: "What difficult emotions am I avoiding that need to be addressed?"

➢ Fortitude: "How can I remain emotionally steady during family challenges or conflicts?"

➢ Faith: "How does my trust in God influence my emotional responses?"

> Love: "How can I better demonstrate emotional attunement with each family member?"

Financial Wealth

Financial Wealth refers to your stewardship of material resources and provision for your family's needs. Financial decisions reflect your values and priorities, teaching your children powerful lessons about contentment, generosity, and responsibility. Scripture teaches that "the love of money is a root of all kinds of evil" (1 Timothy 6:10) while also emphasizing the importance of providing for one's family (1 Timothy 5:8).

Your approach to finances shapes your family's security, opportunities, and understanding of stewardship principles.

Assessment Areas:

> **Financial literacy**: Do you understand basic financial principles and actively manage your resources?

> **Budgeting and planning**: Have you established clear financial goals and a budget that aligns with your family values?

> **Debt management**: Are you working toward financial freedom through responsible debt reduction?

> **Generosity practices**: How are you modeling cheerful giving? "Each of you should give what you have decided in your heart to give, not reluctantly or under compulsion, for God loves a cheerful giver" (2 Corinthians 9:7).

> **Financial communication**: How openly and constructively do you discuss money matters with your spouse and children?

Reflection Questions:

> Courage: "What financial realities am I avoiding that need to be addressed?"

> Fortitude: "How can I maintain financial discipline even when facing temptations or pressures?"

> Faith: "How can I demonstrate greater trust in God's provision while practicing responsible stewardship?"

> Love: "How can my financial decisions better reflect love for my family and others?"

Self-Reflection Integration: Identifying Your Wealth Foundation Priorities

Having examined your emotional and financial wealth, it's time to identify the specific areas requiring focused attention. This prioritization process helps transform insights into actionable growth opportunities that strengthen your fatherhood effectiveness.

Priority Selection Process

For each wealth foundation area (emotional and financial), select 2-3 specific aspects that:

> ➢ Most significantly impact your family's well-being and your effectiveness as a father

> ➢ Align with your personal fatherhood vision

> ➢ Currently present the most significant gap between your current state and your desired state

> ➢ Would create positive ripple effects across multiple areas of your family life

Remember: Meaningful growth comes from focused effort on your most important opportunities, not trying to address everything simultaneously. Consider which core virtue (courage, fortitude, faith, or love) will be essential for progress in each area.

Looking Ahead: From Wealth to Family Connections

As you complete Day 4 of your Fatherhood Awakening journey, take a moment to recognize the significant work you've accomplished. By honestly assessing your emotional and financial wealth, you've identified specific areas where growth will strengthen your foundation as a father. These insights represent not weaknesses but opportunities—each one is a stepping stone toward becoming the father your family needs.

Remember that this process isn't about achieving perfection but about intentional growth. Small, consistent improvements in managing your emotions and finances will benefit your entire family. As Proverbs 21:5 reminds us, "The plans of the diligent lead to profit as surely as haste leads to poverty."

Priority Documentation Template

Emotional Wealth Priorities

Priority:

Current reality:

Desired state:

Core virtue needed:

Priority:

Current reality:

Desired state:

Core virtue needed:

Priority:

Current reality:

Desired state:

Core virtue needed:

Financial Wealth Priorities

Priority:

Current reality:

Desired state:

Core virtue needed:

Priority:

Current reality

Desired state:

Core virtue needed:

Priority:

Current reality:

Desired state

Core virtue needed:

Preparing for Day 5: The Heart of Fatherhood

Tomorrow, we'll move from the foundational elements of health and wealth to the heart of your fatherhood journey—family relationships. Day 5 focuses on two critical foundational strengths: your marriage relationship and your connection with your children.

These relationships represent both your greatest responsibility and your greatest opportunity for impact. How you love your spouse teaches your children about commitment, respect, and authentic love. How you connect with your children shapes their sense of worth, security, and identity for a lifetime.

As you prepare for tomorrow's important work, consider these words from Joshua 1:9: "Have I not commanded you? Be strong and courageous. Do not be afraid; do not be discouraged, for the LORD your God will be with you wherever you go." The same courage and fortitude you've applied to examine your health and wealth foundations will serve you well as you honestly assess these vital relationships.

Tonight, take a few moments to pray specifically for wisdom and clarity as you prepare to examine these most precious aspects of your life. The awareness and intentionality you bring to tomorrow's reflections will set the stage for transformative growth in your family relationships.

Your commitment to this process is a powerful testament to your love for your family. Press on—the most meaningful work awaits.

Notes

Day 5: Family Foundation - Marriage and Parent-Child Connections

Welcome to Day 5 of your Fatherhood Awakening journey, where we focus on the heart of your family ecosystem: marriage and relationships with your children. These two foundational strengths form the core of your family identity and determine the emotional climate of your home. Today's reflections will help you identify areas where intentional growth can transform your family dynamics and deepen your most important relationships.

As you engage with these sensitive and profound areas, approach them with both honesty and grace. Remember that acknowledging growth opportunities in these relationships isn't about dwelling on shortcomings but embracing the potential for greater connection, understanding, and love.

Marriage Relationship

Your Marriage Relationship is the foundation of your family structure and provides the primary model of love your children observe daily. Scripture elevates this relationship with profound significance: "Husbands, love your wives, just as Christ loved the church and gave himself up for her" (Ephesians 5:25). The quality of your marriage directly impacts your effectiveness as a father and shapes your children's understanding of healthy relationships.

A thriving marriage creates a secure environment where children can flourish, while a struggling marriage affects the entire family ecosystem. Your intentional investment in this relationship yields dividends across generations.

Assessment Areas:

> - **Communication patterns**: How effectively do you and your spouse share thoughts, feelings, and needs? Do you practice active listening?

> - **Conflict resolution**: Do you address disagreements constructively, or do you avoid difficult conversations?

> - **Emotional intimacy**: How well do you understand and connect with your spouse's inner world?

> - **Physical intimacy**: Are you nurturing physical closeness and affection in appropriate ways?

- **Shared vision**: Do you and your spouse regularly discuss and align on family priorities and parenting approaches?
- **Appreciation practices**: How consistently do you express gratitude and admiration for your spouse, especially in front of your children?

Reflection Questions:

- Courage: "What difficult conversations or issues am I avoiding in my marriage that must be addressed?"
- Fortitude: "How can I remain committed to serving and honoring my spouse during challenging seasons?"
- Faith: "How can I better reflect Christ's sacrificial love in treating my spouse?"
- Love: "What actions would make my spouse feel more valued and understood?"

Parent-Child Connection

Your Parent-Child Connection forms the foundation where your children's character, identity, and worldview take shape. These relationships represent both your greatest responsibility and your most profound opportunity to leave a lasting legacy. Scripture reminds us, "Start children off on the way they should go, and even when they are old, they will not turn from it" (Proverbs 22:6).

The quality of your connection with each child directly influences their emotional security, self-worth, and capacity for healthy relationships throughout life. Each child requires an individualized approach that honors their unique personality, needs, and love language.

Assessment Areas:

- **Quality time**: Are you consistently present and engaged with each child in meaningful ways?
- **Emotional attunement**: How well do you understand and respond to each child's emotional needs?
- **Communication**: Do you create safe spaces for open dialogue? "My dear brothers and sisters, take note of this: Everyone should be quick to listen, slow to speak, and slow to become angry" (James 1:19).
- **Discipline approach**: Does your discipline balance accountability with grace, focusing on heart change rather than behavior modification?

- ➢ **Affirmation practices**: How effectively do you communicate value and belief in each child's potential?

- ➢ **Individual connection**: Do you know and connect with each child's unique interests, strengths, and challenges?

Reflection Questions:

- ➢ Courage: "What difficult parenting issues am I avoiding that must be addressed?"

- ➢ Fortitude: "How can I remain consistent in my parenting approach even when tired or stressed?"

- ➢ Faith: "How can I better demonstrate God's unconditional love and grace to my children?"

- ➢ Love: "What specific actions would help each of my children feel more secure in my love?"

Self-Reflection Integration: Identifying Your Family Foundation Priorities

Having examined your marriage and parent-child relationships, it's time to identify the specific areas requiring focused attention. This prioritization process helps transform insights into actionable growth opportunities that strengthen your family's core relationships.

Priority Selection Process

For each foundational strength area (marriage relationship and connecting with your children), select 2-3 specific aspects that:

1. Have the most significant impact on your effectiveness as a father

2. Align with your personal fatherhood vision

3. Currently present the most significant gap between your current state and your desired state

4. Would create positive ripple effects across multiple areas of your fatherhood

Remember: Effective growth comes not from trying to improve everything simultaneously but from focused effort on your most important opportunities. As you identify these priorities, consider which core virtue (courage, fortitude, faith, or love) you must emphasize to progress in each area.

Priority Documentation Template

For each foundational strength, complete the following:

Marriage Relationship Priorities

Priority:

Current reality:

Desired state:

Core virtue needed:

Priority:

Current reality:

Desired state:

Core virtue needed:

Priority:

Current reality:

Desired state:

Core virtue needed:

Parent-Child Connection Priorities

Priority:

Current reality

Desired state:

Core virtue needed:

Priority:

Current reality:

Desired state:

Core virtue needed:

Priority:

Current reality:

Desired state:

Core virtue needed:

As you complete Day 5 of your Fatherhood Awakening journey, take a moment to honor the profound work you've accomplished. By examining your marriage and parent-child relationships with honesty and intentionality, you've demonstrated remarkable courage. These relationships form the heart of your family ecosystem, and the growth priorities you've identified will create ripples of positive change for generations to come.

Notes

Day 6: From Reflection to Action - Creating SMART Goals

Congratulations on completing the most challenging part of your Fatherhood Awakening journey. Over the past five days, you've engaged in profound self-examination that many men never dare to undertake. You've crafted a personal fatherhood vision that captures your highest aspirations. You've assessed your current reality across six foundational strengths—physical health, spiritual health, emotional wealth, financial wealth, marriage relationship, and parent-child connections. And you've identified specific growth priorities in each area.

This profound work of reflection has prepared you for the pivotal transition that awaits on Day 6: transforming insights into action through purposeful goal-setting.

The Power of Your Commitment

Your work thus far represents more than just self-reflection—it demonstrates your unwavering commitment to your family. By investing this time in honest self-assessment, you've already distinguished yourself from the countless fathers who simply drift through their family responsibilities without intentionality or purpose. Your willingness to examine both strengths and growth areas shows remarkable courage and love for those who matter most.

As Theodore Roosevelt wisely noted, "Nothing in the world is worth having or worth doing unless it means effort, pain, difficulty." Your effort in this process will yield returns far beyond what you can imagine. Your children and grandchildren will experience the ripple effects of your decisions today.

Day 6: Where Transformation Begins

Today represents the moment when reflection transforms into action. You'll craft the priorities you've identified into SMART goals—Specific, Measurable, Achievable, Relevant, and Time-bound objectives that will guide your growth journey. These aren't vague aspirations but concrete targets with clear paths forward.

This goal-setting process will:

> ➢ Focus your energy on your highest-leverage growth opportunities

> ➢ Provide clear metrics to track your progress

> ➢ Break down significant changes into manageable steps

> ➢ Create accountability for consistent action

➢ Align your daily choices with your long-term fatherhood vision

Remember that becoming the father your family needs isn't about perfection—it's about progression.

Preparing Your Heart and Mind

Take time to carefully review the self-assessment results and priorities you identified during Days 3-5. Look across all six foundational strengths and notice which areas consistently appeared as priorities. Which patterns emerge when you compare these priorities against your fatherhood vision?

As you review, consider:

➢ Which 2-3 areas in each strength category showed the largest gaps between your current reality and desired state?

➢ Which priorities, if addressed, would create the most significant positive impact for your family right now?

➢ Which areas align most closely with the core values expressed in your fatherhood vision?

➢ Which priorities require immediate attention due to their time-sensitive nature?

Your goal today is to narrow your focus to your top 5 priority areas across all six strengths. These will become the foundation for creating SMART goals—specific commitments driving meaningful change in your fatherhood journey. Remember, effective transformation comes not from trying to change everything at once but from a strategic focus on your highest-leverage opportunities.

Creating SMART Goals That Transform Your Fatherhood

Now that you've identified your top 5 priority areas, it's time to transform them into actionable SMART goals. Remember, a SMART goal is:

➢ **Specific**: Defines what you will accomplish

➢ **Measurable**: Includes concrete criteria to measure progress

➢ **Achievable**: Challenging yet realistic, given your resources

➢ **Relevant**: Directly connected to your fatherhood vision

➢ **Time-bound**: Has a specific deadline for completion

Prioritizing Your Goals

Before crafting your SMART goals, consider these key questions to ensure you're focusing on what matters most:

1. **Which goals align most closely with your vision statement?** Goals that directly support your core fatherhood vision will create the most meaningful impact and provide stronger motivation during challenging moments.

2. **Which would create the most positive change for your family?** Consider which goals, if achieved, would significantly improve your family's well-being or address current pain points.

3. **Which feels most urgent or essential right now?** Some goals may address immediate needs that shouldn't be postponed, such as repairing damaged relationships or addressing health concerns.

4. **Which builds a foundation for other goals?** Specific goals create a foundation that makes other goals more straightforward to achieve. For example, improving your physical health often increases energy for other priorities.

Examples of SMART Goals by Category

Physical Health

➢ Vague goal: Get in better shape

➢ SMART goal: Complete 30 minutes of exercise 4 days per week for the next 3 months, including at least 2 strength training sessions weekly, to model healthy habits for my children and have energy for family activities.

Spiritual Health

➢ Vague goal: Develop a better prayer life

➢ SMART goal: Establish a 15-minute morning prayer and scripture reading routine 5 days per week for the next 60 days, including keeping a spiritual journal that I review weekly to track insights and growth.

Emotional Wealth

Vague goal: Be less reactive with my kids

SMART goal: Practice the pause-breathe-respond technique during challenging parenting moments, reducing emotional outbursts by 50% over the next 2 months as measured by a daily evening reflection log.

Financial Wealth
  ➢ Vague goal: Save more money

  ➢ SMART goal: Create and implement a family budget by May 1st that includes automatically transferring $400 monthly to our children's education fund and **reducing discretionary spending by 15%.**

Marriage Relationship
  ➢ Vague goal: Spend more time with my spouse

  ➢ SMART goal: Schedule and protect a 2-hour date night every week for the next 3 months, with phones off and a commitment to discuss one meaningful topic about our relationship or family vision each time.

Parent-Child Connection
  ➢ Vague goal: Be more present with my kids

  ➢ SMART goal: Establish a 20-minute one-on-one connection time with each child 3 times weekly for the next 60 days, where I engage in their chosen activity with no phone or distractions present.

Your Top 5 SMART Goals Worksheet

For each of your top 5 priority areas, complete the following framework:

1. **SMART Goal:** (Write your specific, measurable, achievable, relevant, and time-bound goal)

2. **Why it matters to you and your children:** (Connect this goal to your vision and the impact it will have on your family's well-being)

3. **Target date for achieving it:** (Set a specific deadline that creates healthy urgency)

4. **First action step to take:** (Identify one concrete action you can take within the next 48 hours to build momentum)

Example Completed Worksheet:

SMART Goal #1: Establish a consistent bedtime routine where I read to my children for 15 minutes each night, 5 nights per week for the next 2 months.

Why it matters: This creates quality connection time, builds their literacy skills, and ensures I'm present during an important transition in their day. It fulfills my vision of being emotionally available and investing in their development.

Target date: June 15

First action step: Select 3 age-appropriate books from our shelf or library and place them by their beds tonight. Block out 7:30-8:00 pm in my calendar as "Kids' Bedtime Reading" for the next week.

Your Personal SMART Goals Action Plan

Use the template below to document each of your top 5 SMART goals. Complete all sections for each goal before moving to the next one. This document will serve as your roadmap for transformation over the coming months.

Goal #1

SMART Goal:

Why it matters:

Target date:

First action step:

Potential obstacles:

Strategy to overcome obstacles:

Goal #2

SMART Goal:

Why it matters:

Target date:

First action step:

Potential obstacles:

Strategy to overcome obstacles:

Goal #3

SMART Goal:

Why it matters:

Target date:

First action step:

Potential obstacles:

Strategy to overcome obstacles:

Goal #4

SMART Goal:

Why it matters:

Target date:

First action step:

Potential obstacles:

Strategy to overcome obstacles:

Goal #5

SMART Goal:

Why it matters:

Target date:

First action step:

Potential obstacles:

Strategy to overcome obstacles:

Accountability Plan

Who will I share these goals with?

How often will I review my progress?

What reward will I give myself when I achieve each goal?

How will I get back on track if I fall behind?

Celebrating Your Journey: The Milestone of Completion

Congratulations, father. Take a moment to acknowledge the significant work you've accomplished over these past six days. You've embarked on a journey that few men have the courage to undertake—a deep, honest examination of your fatherhood that has culminated in a concrete action plan for transformation.

In just six days, you have:

> - Crafted a personal fatherhood vision that captures your highest aspirations

> - Honestly assessed your current reality across six foundational strengths

> - Identified specific growth priorities that will create the greatest impact

> - Transformed those priorities into SMART goals with clear action steps

> - Created accountability structures to ensure your continued progress

This work represents far more than completed exercises or written goals—it demonstrates your unwavering commitment to becoming the father your family deserves. Each reflection, each honest assessment, and each carefully crafted goal reflects your love for your children and your dedication to their flourishing.

Notes

Day 7: The Gift of Rest and Reflection

Today marks Day 7 of your Fatherhood Awakening journey—a sacred day of rest and reflection. Just as the seventh day in creation was set aside for rest (Genesis 2:2-3), today is your opportunity to pause, breathe, and allow the insights of the past week to integrate fully into your being.

As you prepare for today, know that your work has already set powerful changes in motion. The father who began this process six days ago is not the same man who completes it today. **You've awakened to a new level of awareness, purpose, and responsibility.**

The SMART goals you've created are not just tasks to complete—they're stepping stones on the path to becoming the father you're called to be. Each goal you achieve will build momentum for the next, creating a positive cycle of growth that will transform not only your fatherhood but your entire family legacy, for "as for me and my house, we will serve the LORD" (Joshua 24:15).

Take pride in what you've accomplished. Know that this Fatherhood Awakening journey is just beginning—the most rewarding chapters still lie ahead, waiting to be written through your daily choices and unwavering commitment to growth, for "train up a child in the way he should go; even when he is old he will not depart from it" (Proverbs 22:6).

Your children's future selves are already thanking you for the father you're becoming today.

Sacred Rest and Strategic Reflection

After six days of intense self-examination and planning, today is set apart for something equally important: rest and prayerful reflection. Just as the Creator rested on the seventh day, you, too, need this sacred pause to integrate all you've learned and prepare your heart for the implementation phase ahead.

The Power of Sacred Rest

This day of rest isn't about inactivity but intentional reflection. Take time today to sit quietly with your completed work. Review your fatherhood vision statement slowly, allowing each word to resonate with your spirit. Consider how this vision captures the essence of the father you're becoming.

Revisit your top 5 priority areas and the SMART goals you've created. As you review them with fresh eyes and a rested mind, you may notice new insights or connections that weren't apparent during the initial work. This is the gift of reflection—seeing with greater clarity after stepping back from the details.

Prayer and Discernment

Set aside dedicated time today for prayer about your fatherhood journey. Ask for:

- ➤ **Wisdom** to know which goal deserves your first attention, for "if any of you lacks wisdom, let him ask God, who gives generously to all without reproach" (James 1:5)

- ➤ **Courage** to face the growth areas that feel most challenging, remembering that "I can do all things through him who strengthens me" (Philippians 4:13)

- ➤ **Humility** to receive help when needed, for "God opposes the proud but gives grace to the humble" (1 Peter 5:5)

- ➤ **Fortitude** when progress feels slow, knowing that "let us not grow weary of doing good, for in due season we will reap if we do not give up" (Galatians 6:9)

- ➤ **Love** for the opportunity to grow as a father, for "every good gift and every perfect gift is from above" (James 1:17)

This prayerful reflection will help you discern what to do and where to begin. Not all goals, even SMART ones, are created equal. Some will build a foundation that makes others easier to achieve. Others may address urgent family needs that shouldn't wait.

Prioritizing Your First Steps

As you review your 5 SMART goals, consider these questions to determine where to begin:

- ➤ Which goal, if achieved, would create momentum for several others?

- ➤ Which addresses the most immediate need in your family?

- ➤ Which aligns most directly with your core values expressed in your vision?

- ➤ Which would be most noticeable to your children if achieved?

- ➤ Which feels most energizing to you right now?

The wisdom of fatherhood growth lies not in trying to transform everything at once but in making small, consistent steps in the right direction. Choose just 1-2 goals to focus on initially. Master these before adding others. This incremental approach builds confidence, creates visible wins, and establishes sustainable patterns.

Preparing for the 30-Day Journey Ahead

Tomorrow, you'll begin a 30-day devotional and journaling practice designed to reinforce and build upon the foundation you've established this week. Each day's reflection will provide guidance, encouragement, and practical wisdom for your fatherhood journey.

Allow these daily touchpoints to keep your vision and goals at the forefront of your mind. The devotional isn't separate from your SMART goals—the daily nourishment will fuel your progress.

Weekly Check-In Plan

Sustainable growth requires regular assessment. Establish a weekly review ritual—perhaps Sunday evening or Monday morning—to evaluate your progress and recalibrate as needed. During this weekly check-in:

1. Review your fatherhood vision statement
2. Assess progress on your active SMART goals
3. Identify any obstacles that arise and strategize solutions
4. Celebrate small wins and progress, no matter how incremental
5. Adjust timelines or approaches if necessary
6. Identify one key focus for the coming week

This weekly practice will help you maintain momentum while providing flexibility to adapt to your family's changing needs and circumstances. To support this process, the 30-day devotional and journal includes a weekly check-in template at the end of each week, giving you a structured format to reflect on your progress and plan your next steps.

The Art of Elimination and Delegation

Becoming a better father isn't just about adding new practices—it's also about eliminating activities that drain your energy without contributing to your family's well-being. During your weekly check-ins, ask yourself:

➢ What activities consumed my time this week but added no value to my fatherhood?

➢ Which responsibilities could be delegated to create more space for priority relationships?

➢ What good but non-essential commitments might need to be declined to protect family time?

➤ How can I simplify our family schedule to reduce stress and increase connection?

The courage to say no to the non-essential creates the space to say yes to what matters most. This disciplined elimination is often the hidden key to fatherhood transformation, for "there is a time for everything, and a season for every activity under the heavens" (Ecclesiastes 3:1).

Celebrating the Beginning

Today marks not an ending but a beginning. Completing this week's work represents the foundation upon which you'll build a legacy of intentional, purposeful fatherhood. Take time today to celebrate the courage it took to engage in this profound work of self-examination and planning. Few fathers ever invest this level of thought and care into their most important role.

If you have not done so already, now is a good time to connect with other fathers on the same journey. Consider joining the Fathering Strong network of dads working to be the best fathers they can be for their families and communities. This is a free community full of valuable resources. You can also connect with like-minded dads and travel down this invaluable path of fatherhood together, for "iron sharpens iron, and one man sharpens another" (Proverbs 27:17). Consider joining Fathering Strong today at www.fatheringstrong.com.

Fathering Strong Blueprint Summary

Fatherhood Vision

Virtue Assessment Ranking

Virtue	Courage	Fortitude	Faith	Love
Ranking				

Core Strength Ranking

Top Priority	

Top SMART Goals

Priority	Goal	Why it matters	Achieve By	First Action
1				
2				
3				
4				
5				

Accountability Partner:	
Next Check-in Date:	

Notes

PART 2: 30-Day Devotional and Journal

The power of this devotional comes from how you engage with it each day. Before starting this journey, let's explore how to make the most of your daily practice to create lasting change in your role as a father.

Creating Your Sacred Space

The environment for your devotional time matters deeply. Find a space - whether it's a quiet corner in your home office, a comfortable chair in your bedroom, or even your favorite local coffee shop - that allows you to focus without distraction. Make it an inviting place and naturally encourage reflection, prayer, and honest self-examination.

Setting up your space with purpose can enhance your experience. Keep your essentials close by: your Bible, journal, and a reliable pen. Many dads find that adding personal touches, like peaceful background music and a fresh cup of coffee helps create an atmosphere that signals to both mind and spirit.

Establishing Your Rhythm

While the devotional provides structure, developing your rhythm within that structure is crucial. Some fathers prefer to begin their day with reflection, finding that early morning quiet provides the mental clarity needed for deep engagement. Others discover that evening reflection allows them to process the day's experiences and prepare their hearts for tomorrow.

The key isn't the specific time you choose but rather your commitment to consistency. Your devotional time should become as natural as brushing your teeth – an essential part of your daily routine that you wouldn't think of skipping.

Understanding the Daily Format

Each day's entry has been carefully crafted to guide you through a meaningful engagement with God's Word and your role as a father. The format includes several key components designed to work together for maximum impact.

The **Scripture Focus** is your foundation, providing God's eternal truth as the basis for your growth. Take time to read these passages slowly, perhaps even multiple times. Consider how they specifically apply to your fatherhood journey.

The **Reflection Space** invites you to process what you've read and experienced. Don't rush through this section. Allow yourself to sit with challenging questions and explore your honest responses. Your growth as a father often begins with these moments of genuine self-examination.

The **Action Step** component bridges the gap between insight and implementation. These practical applications help you translate biblical principles into tangible changes in your daily life. While some steps may feel challenging, remember that small, consistent actions create lasting transformation.

The **Prayer Focus** guides you in bringing your fatherhood journey before God. Use this section to develop a deeper prayer life centered on your father role. Your prayers here become powerful declarations of faith and intention.

Maximizing Your Journal Experience

The journaling component of this devotional isn't merely about recording thoughts – it's about creating a living document of your fatherhood journey. Your journal becomes both a mirror reflecting your current reality and a map guiding your future growth.

When writing in your journal, strive for complete honesty. This is your private space to process both victories and struggles. Don't worry about perfect prose or complete sentences. Focus instead on authentic expression of your thoughts, feelings, and aspirations as a father.

Consider using different colored pens or highlighting systems to track various themes in your journal. You might use one color for prayers, another for insights, and another for action steps. This visual organization can help you review and reflect on your journey over time.

Tracking Your Progress

Growth often happens gradually, making it important to assess your progress regularly. While traditional notebooks offer privacy and a tactile experience, digital tools like Day One or Evernote can be powerful allies in this journey. These apps provide secure, password-protected platforms for your reflections, with the ability to add photos, tags, and even location data to your entries. Both apps feature end-to-end encryption to keep your personal thoughts private and secure.

Day One's interface and daily prompts can help maintain your journaling momentum, while its powerful search and tagging features make it easy to track themes and patterns in your growth. Evernote's organizational capabilities allow you to create separate notebooks for different aspects of your journey – prayers, scripture insights, action steps, and family moments. Both apps offer cloud backup, ensuring your reflections are safely preserved even if your device is lost or damaged.

At the end of each week, take time to review your digital entries. Look for patterns, celebrate victories (no matter how small), and identify areas that still need attention. Both apps allow you to easily review past entries by date or tag, helping you see your progress over time.

Consider photographing special moments that illustrate your growth – a morning devotional time with your children, a family dinner where you implemented a new insight, or a tender moment with your spouse. These easily stored and organized visual reminders in your chosen app can encourage you on challenging days.

Building in Accountability

While this journey is personal, it shouldn't be solitary. Consider sharing your commitment with your spouse, a trusted friend, or a group of fellow fathers. Regular check-ins with an accountability partner can provide encouragement, insight, and motivation to stay consistent with your daily practice.

The Fathering Strong app provides additional opportunities for connection and accountability. Use its features to connect with other fathers on similar journeys, share insights, and encourage one another in growth.

Handling Missed Days

There will likely be days when life's demands prevent you from completing your devotional. When this happens, extend yourself grace while maintaining commitment. Rather than trying to catch up by doing multiple days at once, simply resume with the current day's entry. The goal is progress, not perfection.

Creating Lasting Change

As you progress through this devotional, remember that lasting change happens through small, consistent steps rather than dramatic gestures. Each day's engagement with this material plants seeds that will grow into stronger fatherhood practices over time.

Pay attention to how your children and spouse respond to the changes they observe in you. Their reactions can provide valuable feedback and encouragement as you continue your growth journey.

Looking Beyond 30 Days

While this devotional spans 30 days, consider it a launching pad for lifelong growth as a father. The habits and insights you develop during this time can become the foundation for continued intentional fatherhood long after you complete the final entry.

Many fathers revisit this devotional annually, finding new insights and applications with each pass through the material. Others use it as a springboard to develop ongoing reflection and growth practices.

Your Legacy in the Making

Remember that every moment you spend engaging with this devotional is an investment in your family's future. The insights you gain, the prayers you pray, and the changes you implement create ripples that will impact future generations.

Approach each day's entry with expectancy and commitment, knowing that God is faithful to meet you in these moments of intentional growth. Your dedication to becoming a stronger father matters more than you know, and this devotional stands ready to guide you on that transformative journey.

Your Weekly Path to Stronger Fatherhood

Success in any journey requires not just a destination but a consistent way to check your progress and adjust your course. As you develop your path to stronger fatherhood, establishing a weekly rhythm of reflection and adjustment becomes crucial. This structured approach helps you stay accountable to your vision while allowing the flexibility to adapt to your family's changing needs.

The Value of Regular Check-ins

The path to becoming a better father isn't linear — it's a dynamic journey that requires ongoing evaluation and refinement. James, a father of two, shares his experience: "When I first started, I thought having a plan was enough. But it wasn't until I committed to weekly check-ins that I saw real change. These regular reviews helped me spot patterns, celebrate progress, and course-correct before small issues become major obstacles."

Your weekly check-ins serve as navigation points, helping you stay aligned with your vision while making necessary adjustments. Think of them as regular maintenance for your fatherhood journey — moments to refuel your motivation, repair what isn't working, and recommit to your most important priorities.

The Weekly Check-In Process

Setting goals is just the first step. Success comes through consistent review and refinement of your progress. To help you maintain momentum, we've created a Weekly Check-In template available at fatheringstrongbook.com. This practical tool guides you through reflecting on your achievements and challenges while planning for the week ahead.

The Weekly Check-In template includes four essential components designed to keep you focused and intentional in your fatherhood journey:

1. **Vision Statement Review:** Begin by reconnecting with your fatherhood vision statement. This grounding exercise ensures your daily actions align with your long-term goals and values for your family.

2. **Weekly Reflection:** Take time to document both challenges and victories from the past week. What moments made you proud? Where did you face difficulties? This honest assessment helps identify patterns and opportunities for growth.

3. **Upcoming Week Focus:** Map out your key priorities and commitments for the week ahead. Be specific about how you'll allocate your time and energy to ensure your most important relationships receive adequate attention.

4. **Connection and Growth Plan:** Detail concrete ways to nurture relationships with your children and spouse this week. Include specific activities, quality time commitments, and intentional conversations. Additionally, outline your personal growth goals, including spiritual development, physical health, and emotional well-being.

David, a father of two, discovered the power of this approach: "The weekly check-in revolutionized my fatherhood journey. Using the template helped me track my progress and identify tasks I needed to delegate or eliminate. I learned that saying 'no' to good things allowed me to say 'yes' to the best things for my family."

Creating Your Weekly Review Rhythm

Choose a consistent time each week for your review. Many fathers find Sunday evening ideal, allowing them to reflect on the past week and prepare for the week ahead. Find a quiet space where you can think deeply without interruption.

Begin your review with prayer and gratitude. Thank God for specific moments of connection with your children from the past week. Acknowledge His presence in your fatherhood journey and invite His wisdom into your reflection process.

Adjusting Your Approach

Use insights from your reflection to adjust your approach for the coming week. Perhaps you need to modify a goal's timeline or break it down into smaller steps. Maybe you've identified a new resource or support system that could help you succeed.

Michael's experience illustrates this well: "I realized my goal of morning devotions wasn't working because I was trying to do it too early. I finally found a rhythm that stuck by adjusting the timing right after breakfast."

Planning for Success

End your weekly check-in by setting specific intentions for the week ahead. Review your top ten goals and identify which ones need particular attention. Create concrete action steps and schedule them into your calendar.

Consider potential obstacles and plan how you'll handle them. If you know a busy work week is coming, how will you protect your family connection time? If certain situations typically trigger impatience, what strategies will you employ to stay calm?

Maintaining Momentum Through Accountability

Weekly check-ins gain extra power when you share them with an accountability partner - whether your spouse, a trusted friend, or another father walking a similar path. Regular conversations about wins, struggles, and course corrections help maintain your focus and motivate you.

As Robert discovered: "Meeting with my accountability partner every other week helped me stay honest about my progress. His questions and encouragement kept me moving forward, even when I felt like giving up."

Creating Lasting Change

Remember that meaningful change happens gradually through small, consistent actions taken each day. Your weekly check-ins create a natural rhythm of reflection and adjustment, helping transform your vision of fatherhood into daily reality. Each review session becomes another step toward becoming the father your children need.

As you implement this system of priority goals and weekly reviews, be flexible and kind to yourself. You'll see clear progress some weeks, while others might feel like setbacks. What truly matters is staying committed to the journey and being willing to learn and adjust as you go.

Looking Ahead

Your top five SMART goals and weekly check-in routine create a practical framework for growing as a father. Remember that this system stays flexible – it's meant to evolve with you and your family.

Keep your vision statement in sight during weekly reviews. Let it guide and motivate you as you celebrate wins, learn from setbacks, and fine-tune your approach to purposeful fatherhood. Through this steady rhythm of reflection and action, you're building more than just goals – creating a lasting legacy of love, wisdom, and purpose that will impact generations.

Your Legacy Begins Today - The Power of Intentional Fatherhood

The journey you're about to begin is more than just a 30-day program or a checklist of goals. It's your commitment to creating a legacy that will echo through generations. As you stand at this threshold, ready to dive into daily reflections and intentional growth, understand the profound impact of the path ahead. This journey doesn't end after 30 days — it's a continuous growth cycle. After your first month, you'll revisit your goals, celebrate your wins, adjust your approach where needed, and begin another 30-day cycle. This ongoing commitment ensures your development as a father never stagnates but evolves and strengthens over time.

Take Michael, a father of two who once doubted he had time for structured reflection and goal-setting. "I was always busy providing for my family," he shares. "But I realized I was just spinning my wheels without intentional direction. Setting aside time to work on becoming a better father has been the best investment I've ever made. My children no longer hear my words — they see my commitment to growth in action."

The four foundational virtues — courage, fortitude, faith, and love — serve as your compass throughout this journey.

Courage empowers you to confront uncomfortable truths about areas where you need growth. It gives you the strength to have difficult conversations, set healthy boundaries, and step into leadership even when you feel unprepared. James, a father of three, shares: "It took courage to admit I needed to change my approach to disciplining my children. But that admission became the catalyst for transforming our entire family dynamic."

Fortitude helps you persist when obstacles emerge. The path of intentional fatherhood isn't always smooth — you'll face days when old habits try to resurface, work pressures compete with your commitments, or family crises drain your energy. Your fortitude, built through daily reflection and prayer, keeps you focused during challenging seasons.

Faith anchors your journey in something greater than yourself. It reminds you that you're not alone — the God who entrusted you with your children's care also provides the wisdom and strength to raise them well. Through faith, you learn to trust the process, even when progress feels slow or setbacks occur.

Love brings purpose and meaning to every aspect of your fatherhood journey. It transforms routine tasks into moments of connection, discipline into discipleship, and daily challenges into opportunities to show unconditional acceptance. As Thomas, a veteran father of four, reflects: "When love became my motivation rather than obligation, everything changed. My children responded differently because they could feel the difference in my approach."

The SMART goals you'll set throughout this journey serve as practical stepping stones toward your larger vision. Each specific, measurable, achievable, relevant, and time-bound objective builds momentum for lasting change. Instead of getting overwhelmed by vague aspirations, you'll create clear, actionable steps that naturally progress.

Take Robert's story as an example: "I used to tell myself I needed to 'be more present' with my kids. But nothing changed until I set specific goals: fifteen minutes of undivided attention with each child every evening, no phone during dinner, and weekend activities planned by Wednesday. These concrete steps transformed my relationship with my children."

Your commitment to this journey shows deep wisdom about what truly matters. In a world constantly pulling at your attention and energy, choosing to invest time in becoming a stronger father shows remarkable clarity of purpose. Every minute of reflection, every carefully crafted goal, every small victory celebrated adds to a legacy that will impact generations.

Remember that becoming a better father doesn't require perfection – it requires persistence. You'll have days when you fall short of your ideals, goals seem distant, or old patterns resurface. These moments don't define your journey; how you respond to them reveals your growing character as a father. Each time you choose to begin again, realign with your vision, and pursue your goals with renewed dedication, you model resilience and authenticity for your children.

As you begin your 30-day journey, you join a brotherhood of fathers who've chosen to grow with purpose. Your commitment to strengthening each core area – physical health, spiritual health, emotional wealth, financial wealth, marriage relationships, and father-child bonding – builds a foundation that will impact far beyond your immediate family.

You have all the tools you need to succeed: the self-assessment, SMART goal framework, weekly review process, and daily reflection structure. But your most powerful asset is your committed heart – your daily decision to show up, learn, and become the father your family needs.

Let your vision of the father you want to be *inspire you*. Let the four virtues *guide you*. Let your SMART goals *direct you*. Above all, let love *motivate*

***every step* you take.** Your journey to stronger fatherhood starts now, and its effects will echo through generations.

The next thirty days offer guided reflection, practical wisdom, and chances to grow. Face each day knowing that small, consistent actions create profound change. Your legacy as a father isn't just about reaching a destination – it's about choosing each day to grow, love, and lead with a clear purpose.

This is your moment to embrace your most important role - being a father. Your family's future deserves every ounce of energy you invest in this journey. Trust the process, lean into the challenges, and step forward with confidence. The father you're becoming is exactly who your children need, and each day of this journey will help you unlock that potential.

30-Day Devotional and Journal

Day 1 – Daily Devotional and Journal

Today's Date:

Fathering Strong Daily Focus

Core Strength and Virtue: Physical Health and Courage

Quote: *"The greatest test of courage is to bear defeat without losing heart."* - *Robert Green Ingersoll*

Fatherhood Tip: Take the first step toward better health today by scheduling a complete physical examination. Your children need you to be proactive about your well-being.

Today's Scripture Focus

"I can do all things through Christ who strengthens me." - *Philippians 4:13*

How does this scripture apply to your role as a father?

Personal Reflection Space

What progress did I make yesterday towards my goals?

What is one thing I learned about myself yesterday?

What blessings did I notice yesterday?

Emotional Check-in

How do I feel today?

Why do I feel this way?

How do these emotions affect my parenting?

Daily Action Steps

What are today's primary goals and action plans I will take toward my SMART goals?

What actions will I take today that address the four core virtues of courage, fortitude, faith, and love?

Prayer Focus

What are my prayers for today to grow as a father?

What are my prayers for my children today?

What are my prayers for my marriage and family today?

What other prayers do I have today?

Day 2 – Daily Devotional and Journal

Today's Date:

Fathering Strong Daily Focus

Core Strength and Virtue: Spiritual Health & Faith

Quote: *"A father's faith becomes the map his children follow." – Unknown*

Fatherhood Tip: Begin a morning prayer routine, even if just for five minutes. Your consistent spiritual practice sets a powerful example

Today's Scripture Focus

"Train up a child in the way he should go, and when he is old he will not depart from it." - Proverbs 22:6

How does this scripture apply to your role as a father?

Personal Reflection Space
What progress did I make yesterday towards my goals?

What is one thing I learned about myself yesterday?

What blessings did I notice yesterday?

Emotional Check-in

How do I feel today?

Why do I feel this way?

How do these emotions affect my parenting?

Daily Action Steps

What are today's primary goals and action plans I will take toward my SMART goals?

What actions will I take today that address the four core virtues of courage, fortitude, faith, and love?

Prayer Focus

What are my prayers for today to grow as a father?

What are my prayers for my children today?

What are my prayers for my marriage and family today?

What other prayers do I have today?

Day 3 – Daily Devotional and Journal

Today's Date:

Fathering Strong Daily Focus

Core Strength and Virtue: Emotional Wealth & Love

Quote: *"Children will not remember you for the material things you provided but for the feeling that you cherished them." - Richard L. Evans*

Fatherhood Tip: Practice active listening today. Put down your phone, make eye contact, and fully engage when your children speak.

Today's Scripture Focus

"Love is patient, love is kind..." - 1 Corinthians 13:4

How does this scripture apply to your role as a father?

Personal Reflection Space
What progress did I make yesterday towards my goals?

What is one thing I learned about myself yesterday?

What blessings did I notice yesterday?

Emotional Check-in

How do I feel today?

Why do I feel this way?

How do these emotions affect my parenting?

Daily Action Steps

What are today's primary goals and action plans I will take toward my SMART goals?

What actions will I take today that address the four core virtues of courage, fortitude, faith, and love?

Prayer Focus

What are my prayers for today to grow as a father?

What are my prayers for my children today?

What are my prayers for my marriage and family today?

What other prayers do I have today?

Day 4– Daily Devotional and Journal

Today's Date:

Fathering Strong Daily Focus

Core Strength and Virtue: Financial Wealth and Fortitude

Quote: *"The greatest legacy we can leave our children is not money, but character." - Billy Graham*

Fatherhood Tip: Start a college savings plan for your children today. Financial planning shows both love and responsibility.

Today's Scripture Focus

"Whoever loves money never has enough; whoever loves wealth is never satisfied with their income." - Ecclesiastes 5:10

How does this scripture apply to your role as a father?

Personal Reflection Space

What progress did I make yesterday towards my goals?

What is one thing I learned about myself yesterday?

What blessings did I notice yesterday?

Emotional Check-in

How do I feel today?

Why do I feel this way?

How do these emotions affect my parenting?

Daily Action Steps

What are today's primary goals and action plans I will take toward my SMART goals?

What actions will I take today that address the four core virtues of courage, fortitude, faith, and love?

Prayer Focus

What are my prayers for today to grow as a father?

What are my prayers for my children today?

What are my prayers for my marriage and family today?

What other prayers do I have today?

Day 5 – Daily Devotional and Journal

Today's Date:

Fathering Strong Daily Focus

Core Strength and Virtue: Physical Health & Love

Quote: *"The best gift you can give your family is a healthy you." – Unknown*

Fatherhood Tip: Invite your children to exercise with you. Make physical activity a bonding experience.

Today's Scripture Focus

"Do you not know that your bodies are temples of the Holy Spirit?" - 1 Corinthians 6:19

How does this scripture apply to your role as a father?

Personal Reflection Space

What progress did I make yesterday towards my goals?

What is one thing I learned about myself yesterday?

What blessings did I notice yesterday?

Emotional Check-in

How do I feel today?

Why do I feel this way?

How do these emotions affect my parenting?

Daily Action Steps

What are today's primary goals and action plans I will take toward my SMART goals?

What actions will I take today that address the four core virtues of courage, fortitude, faith, and love?

Prayer Focus

What are my prayers for today to grow as a father?

What are my prayers for my children today?

What are my prayers for my marriage and family today?

What other prayers do I have today?

Day 6 – Daily Devotional and Journal

Today's Date:

Fathering Strong Daily Focus

Core Strength and Virtue: Marriage Relationships & Faith

Quote: *"A good marriage isn't something you find; it's something you make."* *- Gary Thomas*

Fatherhood Tip: Pray with your spouse today. Shared faith strengthens marital bonds

Today's Scripture Focus

"Two are better than one because they have a good return for their labor." - *Ecclesiastes 4:9*

How does this scripture apply to your role as a father?

Personal Reflection Space

What progress did I make yesterday towards my goals?

What is one thing I learned about myself yesterday?

What blessings did I notice yesterday?

Emotional Check-in

How do I feel today?

Why do I feel this way?

How do these emotions affect my parenting?

Daily Action Steps

What are today's primary goals and action plans I will take toward my SMART goals?

What actions will I take today that address the four core virtues of courage, fortitude, faith, and love?

Prayer Focus

What are my prayers for today to grow as a father?

What are my prayers for my children today?

What are my prayers for my marriage and family today?

What other prayers do I have today?

Day 7 – Daily Devotional and Journal

Today's Date:

Fathering Strong Daily Focus

Core Strength and Virtue: Father-Child Bonding & Courage

Quote: *"It takes courage to raise children, but children raise our courage." – Unknown*

Fatherhood Tip: Face a fear alongside your child today. Show them how to be brave.

Today's Scripture Focus

"Be strong and courageous. Do not be terrified; do not be discouraged." - Joshua 1:9

How does this scripture apply to your role as a father?

Personal Reflection Space

What progress did I make yesterday towards my goals?

What is one thing I learned about myself yesterday?

What blessings did I notice yesterday?

Emotional Check-in

How do I feel today?

Why do I feel this way?

How do these emotions affect my parenting?

Daily Action Steps

What are today's primary goals and action plans I will take toward my SMART goals?

What actions will I take today that address the four core virtues of courage, fortitude, faith, and love?

Prayer Focus

What are my prayers for today to grow as a father?

What are my prayers for my children today?

What are my prayers for my marriage and family today?

What other prayers do I have today?

Week 1 - Check-In Plan

Vision Statement Review

Do I feel this week's actions aligned with my vision statement? Why or why not?

What changes do I need to make to my vision statement?

Last Week Reflection

What wins can I celebrate?

What challenges did I face?

What Lessons did I learn?

This Week's SMART Goal Focus

SMART Goals	Why this goal matters	Actions I will take

Resource Management

What am I doing that I can delegate this week?

What can I simplify or reprioritize to provide more time to focus on my SMART goals?

What am I currently doing that I can eliminate?

Quality Time Planning With My Children

Child's Name   Activity Planned   When Scheduled

Family Connection Activities I Plan for This Week

Planned Family Activities   When?

What family spiritual focus activities do I plan for this week

Self-care & Growth

What activities will I do this week to continue to grow as a father?

What activities will I do this week to improve my health?

What activities will I do this week to improve my spiritual growth?

Weekly Prayer

What will be my prayer focus for this week?

Notes & Ideas

What additional thoughts, inspirations, or reminders should I document for this week?

Day 8 – Daily Devotional and Journal

Today's Date:

Fathering Strong Daily Focus

Core Strength and Virtue: Emotional Wealth & Fortitude

Quote: *"The strongest people are not those who show strength in front of us but those who win battles we know nothing about." – Unknown*

Fatherhood Tip: Share a personal struggle you've overcome with your children. Let them see your resilience.

Today's Scripture Focus

"A patient man has great understanding." - Proverbs 14:29

How does this scripture apply to your role as a father?

Personal Reflection Space

What progress did I make yesterday towards my goals?

What is one thing I learned about myself yesterday?

What blessings did I notice yesterday?

Emotional Check-in

How do I feel today?

Why do I feel this way?

How do these emotions affect my parenting?

Daily Action Steps

What are today's primary goals and action plans I will take toward my SMART goals?

What actions will I take today that address the four core virtues of courage, fortitude, faith, and love?

Prayer Focus

What are my prayers for today to grow as a father?

What are my prayers for my children today?

What are my prayers for my marriage and family today?

What other prayers do I have today?

Day 9 – Daily Devotional and Journal

Today's Date:

Fathering Strong Daily Focus

Core Strength and Virtue: Spiritual Health & Love

Quote: *"Love is the bridge between you and everything." - Rumi Fatherhood*

Fatherhood Tip: Write a spiritual blessing for each of your children. Share it with them.

Today's Scripture Focus

"And now these three remain: faith, hope, and love. But the greatest of these is love." - 1 Corinthians 13:13

How does this scripture apply to your role as a father?

Personal Reflection Space

What progress did I make yesterday towards my goals?

What is one thing I learned about myself yesterday?

What blessings did I notice yesterday?

Emotional Check-in

How do I feel today?

Why do I feel this way?

How do these emotions affect my parenting?

Daily Action Steps

What are today's primary goals and action plans I will take toward my SMART goals?

What actions will I take today that address the four core virtues of courage, fortitude, faith, and love?

Prayer Focus

What are my prayers for today to grow as a father?

What are my prayers for my children today?

What are my prayers for my marriage and family today?

What other prayers do I have today?

Day 10 – Daily Devotional and Journal

Today's Date:

Fathering Strong Daily Focus

Core Strength and Virtue: Financial Wealth & Faith

Quote: *"Money is a terrible master but an excellent servant." - P.T. Barnum*

Fatherhood Tip: Teach your children about tithing and charitable giving today

Today's Scripture Focus

"For where your treasure is, there your heart will be also." - Matthew 6:21:4

How does this scripture apply to your role as a father?

Personal Reflection Space

What progress did I make yesterday towards my goals?

What is one thing I learned about myself yesterday?

What blessings did I notice yesterday?

Emotional Check-in

How do I feel today?

Why do I feel this way?

How do these emotions affect my parenting?

Daily Action Steps

What are today's primary goals and action plans I will take toward my SMART goals?

What actions will I take today that address the four core virtues of courage, fortitude, faith, and love?

Prayer Focus

What are my prayers for today to grow as a father?

What are my prayers for my children today?

What are my prayers for my marriage and family today?

What other prayers do I have today?

Day 11– Daily Devotional and Journal

Today's Date:

Fathering Strong Daily Focus

Core Strength and Virtue: Physical Health & Fortitude

Quote: *"The difference between try and triumph is just a little umph!"* - *Marvin Phillips*

Fatherhood Tip: Set a physical challenge for yourself and your family. Persevere together.

Today's Scripture Focus

"But those who hope in the Lord will renew their strength." - *Isaiah 40:*

How does this scripture apply to your role as a father?

Personal Reflection Space

What progress did I make yesterday towards my goals?

What is one thing I learned about myself yesterday?

What blessings did I notice yesterday?

Emotional Check-in

How do I feel today?

Why do I feel this way?

How do these emotions affect my parenting?

Daily Action Steps

What are today's primary goals and action plans I will take toward my SMART goals?

What actions will I take today that address the four core virtues of courage, fortitude, faith, and love?

Prayer Focus

What are my prayers for today to grow as a father?

What are my prayers for my children today?

What are my prayers for my marriage and family today?

What other prayers do I have today?

Day 12 – Daily Devotional and Journal

Today's Date:

Fathering Strong Daily Focus

Core Strength and Virtue: Marriage Relationships & Courage

Quote: *"It takes courage to love deeply and show it daily."* – *Unknown*

Fatherhood Tip: Have that difficult conversation you've been avoiding with your spouse. Growth requires courage.

Today's Scripture Focus

"Be completely humble and gentle; be patient, bearing with one another in love." - Ephesians 4:2

How does this scripture apply to your role as a father?

Personal Reflection Space

What progress did I make yesterday towards my goals?

What is one thing I learned about myself yesterday?

What blessings did I notice yesterday?

Emotional Check-in

How do I feel today?

Why do I feel this way?

How do these emotions affect my parenting?

Daily Action Steps

What are today's primary goals and action plans I will take toward my SMART goals?

What actions will I take today that address the four core virtues of courage, fortitude, faith, and love?

Prayer Focus

What are my prayers for today to grow as a father?

What are my prayers for my children today?

What are my prayers for my marriage and family today?

What other prayers do I have today?

Day 13 – Daily Devotional and Journal

Today's Date:

Fathering Strong Daily Focus

Core Strength and Virtue: Father-Child Bonding & Faith

Quote: *"Children are not things to be molded, but people to be unfolded." - Jess Lair*

Fatherhood Tip: Create a family mission statement together. Let faith guide your values.

Today's Scripture Focus

Start children off on the way they should go." - Proverbs 22:6

How does this scripture apply to your role as a father?

Personal Reflection Space
What progress did I make yesterday towards my goals?

What is one thing I learned about myself yesterday?

What blessings did I notice yesterday?

Emotional Check-in

How do I feel today?

Why do I feel this way?

How do these emotions affect my parenting?

Daily Action Steps

What are today's primary goals and action plans I will take toward my SMART goals?

What actions will I take today that address the four core virtues of courage, fortitude, faith, and love?

Prayer Focus

What are my prayers for today to grow as a father?

What are my prayers for my children today?

What are my prayers for my marriage and family today?

What other prayers do I have today?

Day 14 – Daily Devotional and Journal

Today's Date:

Fathering Strong Daily Focus

Core Strength and Virtue: Emotional Wealth & Love

Quote: *"The way we talk to our children becomes their inner voice." - Peggy O'Mara*

Fatherhood Tip: Express three specific things you love about each child today.

Today's Scripture Focus

" Above all else, guard your heart, for everything you do flows from it." - Proverbs 4:23

How does this scripture apply to your role as a father?

Personal Reflection Space

What progress did I make yesterday towards my goals?

What is one thing I learned about myself yesterday?

What blessings did I notice yesterday?

Emotional Check-in

How do I feel today?

Why do I feel this way?

How do these emotions affect my parenting?

Daily Action Steps

What are today's primary goals and action plans I will take toward my SMART goals?

What actions will I take today that address the four core virtues of courage, fortitude, faith, and love?

Prayer Focus

What are my prayers for today to grow as a father?

What are my prayers for my children today?

What are my prayers for my marriage and family today?

What other prayers do I have today?

Week 2 - Check-In Plan

Vision Statement Review

Do I feel this week's actions aligned with my vision statement? Why or why not?

What changes do I need to make to my vision statement?

Last Week Reflection

What wins can I celebrate?

What challenges did I face?

What Lessons did I learn?

This Week's SMART Goal Focus

SMART Goals	Why this goal matters	Actions I will take

Resource Management

What am I doing that I can delegate this week?

What can I simplify or reprioritize to provide more time to focus on my SMART goals?

What am I currently doing that I can eliminate?

Quality Time Planning With My Children

Child's Name   Activity Planned   When Scheduled

Family Connection Activities I Plan for This Week

Planned Family Activities   When?

What family spiritual focus activities do I plan for this week

Self-care & Growth

What activities will I do this week to continue to grow as a father?

What activities will I do this week to improve my health?

What activities will I do this week to improve my spiritual growth?

Weekly Prayer

What will be my prayer focus for this week?

Notes & Ideas

What additional thoughts, inspirations, or reminders should I document for this week?

Day 15 – Daily Devotional and Journal

Today's Date:

Fathering Strong Daily Focus

Core Strength and Virtue: Spiritual Health & Fortitude

Quote: *"Faith is not believing God can, it's knowing He will." – Unknown*

Fatherhood Tip: Share a time when your faith was tested but grew stronger.

Today's Scripture Focus

"Consider it pure joy when you face trials of many kinds." - James 1:2

How does this scripture apply to your role as a father?

Personal Reflection Space

What progress did I make yesterday towards my goals?

What is one thing I learned about myself yesterday?

What blessings did I notice yesterday?

Emotional Check-in

How do I feel today?

Why do I feel this way?

How do these emotions affect my parenting?

Daily Action Steps

What are today's primary goals and action plans I will take toward my SMART goals?

What actions will I take today that address the four core virtues of courage, fortitude, faith, and love?

Prayer Focus

What are my prayers for today to grow as a father?

What are my prayers for my children today?

What are my prayers for my marriage and family today?

What other prayers do I have today?

Day 16 – Daily Devotional and Journal

Today's Date:

Fathering Strong Daily Focus

Core Strength and Virtue: Financial Wealth & Love

Quote: *"True wealth is measured by what we do with what we have." – Unknown*

Fatherhood Tip: Help your children start their first business or savings project.

Today's Scripture Focus

"Give, and it will be given to you." - Luke 6:38

How does this scripture apply to your role as a father?

Personal Reflection Space

What progress did I make yesterday towards my goals?

What is one thing I learned about myself yesterday?

What blessings did I notice yesterday?

Emotional Check-in

How do I feel today?

Why do I feel this way?

How do these emotions affect my parenting?

Daily Action Steps

What are today's primary goals and action plans I will take toward my SMART goals?

What actions will I take today that address the four core virtues of courage, fortitude, faith, and love?

Prayer Focus

What are my prayers for today to grow as a father?

What are my prayers for my children today?

What are my prayers for my marriage and family today?

What other prayers do I have today?

Day 17 – Daily Devotional and Journal

Today's Date:

Fathering Strong Daily Focus

Core Strength and Virtue: Physical Health & Faith

Quote: *"Take care of your body. It's the only place you have to live." - Jim Rohn*

Fatherhood Tip: Bless your meals together. Make the connection between physical and spiritual nourishment.

Today's Scripture Focus

"I praise you because I am fearfully and wonderfully made." - Psalm 139:14

How does this scripture apply to your role as a father?

Personal Reflection Space

What progress did I make yesterday towards my goals?

What is one thing I learned about myself yesterday?

What blessings did I notice yesterday?

Emotional Check-in

How do I feel today?

Why do I feel this way?

How do these emotions affect my parenting?

Daily Action Steps

What are today's primary goals and action plans I will take toward my SMART goals?

What actions will I take today that address the four core virtues of courage, fortitude, faith, and love?

Prayer Focus

What are my prayers for today to grow as a father?

What are my prayers for my children today?

What are my prayers for my marriage and family today?

What other prayers do I have today?

Day 18 – Daily Devotional and Journal

Today's Date:

Fathering Strong Daily Focus

Core Strength and Virtue: Marriage Relationships & Love

Quote: *"A great marriage is not when the perfect couple comes together. It is when an imperfect couple learns to enjoy their differences." - Dave Meurer*

Fatherhood Tip: Write a love letter to your spouse. Let your children see you express affection.

Today's Scripture Focus

"Submit to one another out of reverence for Christ." - Ephesians 5:21

How does this scripture apply to your role as a father?

Personal Reflection Space

What progress did I make yesterday towards my goals?

What is one thing I learned about myself yesterday?

What blessings did I notice yesterday?

Emotional Check-in

How do I feel today?

Why do I feel this way?

How do these emotions affect my parenting?

Daily Action Steps

What are today's primary goals and action plans I will take toward my SMART goals?

What actions will I take today that address the four core virtues of courage, fortitude, faith, and love?

Prayer Focus

What are my prayers for today to grow as a father?

What are my prayers for my children today?

What are my prayers for my marriage and family today?

What other prayers do I have today?

Day 19 – Daily Devotional and Journal

Today's Date:

Fathering Strong Daily Focus

Core Strength and Virtue: Father-Child Bonding & Fortitude

Quote: *"Being a father requires patience, wisdom, and a willingness to make mistakes and learn from them." - Unknown*

Fatherhood Tip: Start a long-term project with your children. Show them the value of persistence.

Today's Scripture Focus

"Let us not become weary in doing good." - Galatians 6:9

How does this scripture apply to your role as a father?

Personal Reflection Space

What progress did I make yesterday towards my goals?

What is one thing I learned about myself yesterday?

What blessings did I notice yesterday?

Emotional Check-in

How do I feel today?

Why do I feel this way?

How do these emotions affect my parenting?

Daily Action Steps

What are today's primary goals and action plans I will take toward my SMART goals?

What actions will I take today that address the four core virtues of courage, fortitude, faith, and love?

Prayer Focus

What are my prayers for today to grow as a father?

What are my prayers for my children today?

What are my prayers for my marriage and family today?

What other prayers do I have today?

Day 20 – Daily Devotional and Journal

Today's Date:

Fathering Strong Daily Focus

Core Strength and Virtue: Emotional Wealth & Courage

Quote: *"Courage is not the absence of fear, but rather the judgment that something else is more important than fear." - Ambrose Redmoon*

Fatherhood Tip: Share your emotions openly today. Show your children it's okay to be vulnerable.

Today's Scripture Focus

"For God has not given us a spirit of fear." - 2 Timothy 1:7

How does this scripture apply to your role as a father?

Personal Reflection Space

What progress did I make yesterday towards my goals?

What is one thing I learned about myself yesterday?

What blessings did I notice yesterday?

Emotional Check-in

How do I feel today?

Why do I feel this way?

How do these emotions affect my parenting?

Daily Action Steps

What are today's primary goals and action plans I will take toward my SMART goals?

What actions will I take today that address the four core virtues of courage, fortitude, faith, and love?

Prayer Focus

What are my prayers for today to grow as a father?

What are my prayers for my children today?

What are my prayers for my marriage and family today?

What other prayers do I have today?

Day 21 – Daily Devotional and Journal

Today's Date:

Fathering Strong Daily Focus

Core Strength and Virtue: Spiritual Health & Faith

Quote: *"Faith is taking the first step even when you don't see the whole staircase." - Martin Luther Jr.*

Fatherhood Tip: Create a family devotional routine that works for your schedule

Today's Scripture Focus

"Seek first his kingdom and his righteousness." - Matthew 6:33

How does this scripture apply to your role as a father?

Personal Reflection Space

What progress did I make yesterday towards my goals?

What is one thing I learned about myself yesterday?

What blessings did I notice yesterday?

Emotional Check-in

How do I feel today?

Why do I feel this way?

How do these emotions affect my parenting?

Daily Action Steps

What are today's primary goals and action plans I will take toward my SMART goals?

What actions will I take today that address the four core virtues of courage, fortitude, faith, and love?

Prayer Focus

What are my prayers for today to grow as a father?

What are my prayers for my children today?

What are my prayers for my marriage and family today?

What other prayers do I have today?

Week 3 - Check-In Plan

Vision Statement Review

Do I feel this week's actions aligned with my vision statement? Why or why not?

What changes do I need to make to my vision statement?

Last Week Reflection

What wins can I celebrate?

What challenges did I face?

What Lessons did I learn?

This Week's SMART Goal Focus

SMART Goals	Why this goal matters	Actions I will take

Resource Management

What am I doing that I can delegate this week?

What can I simplify or reprioritize to provide more time to focus on my SMART goals?

What am I currently doing that I can eliminate?

Quality Time Planning With My Children

Child's Name   **Activity Planned**   **When Scheduled**

Family Connection Activities I Plan for This Week

Planned Family Activities   **When?**

What family spiritual focus activities do I plan for this week

Self-care & Growth

What activities will I do this week to continue to grow as a father?

What activities will I do this week to improve my health?

What activities will I do this week to improve my spiritual growth?

Weekly Prayer

What will be my prayer focus for this week?

Notes & Ideas

What additional thoughts, inspirations, or reminders should I document for this week?

Day 22 – Daily Devotional and Journal

Today's Date:

Fathering Strong Daily Focus

Core Strength and Virtue: Financial Wealth & Courage

Quote: *"It takes courage to live below your means." – Unknown*

Fatherhood Tip: Make a bold financial decision that prioritizes long-term family security.

Today's Scripture Focus

"The wise store up choice food and olive oil, but fools gulp theirs down." - *Proverbs 21:20*

How does this scripture apply to your role as a father?

Personal Reflection Space

What progress did I make yesterday towards my goals?

What is one thing I learned about myself yesterday?

What blessings did I notice yesterday?

Emotional Check-in

How do I feel today?

Why do I feel this way?

How do these emotions affect my parenting?

Daily Action Steps

What are today's primary goals and action plans I will take toward my SMART goals?

What actions will I take today that address the four core virtues of courage, fortitude, faith, and love?

Prayer Focus

What are my prayers for today to grow as a father?

What are my prayers for my children today?

What are my prayers for my marriage and family today?

What other prayers do I have today?

Day 23 – Daily Devotional and Journal

Today's Date:

Fathering Strong Daily Focus

Core Strength and Virtue: Physical Health & Love

Quote: *"Self-care is not selfish. You cannot serve from an empty vessel." - Eleanor Brown*

Fatherhood Tip: Model healthy self-care habits for your children.

Today's Scripture Focus

"Love your neighbor as yourself." - Mark 12:31

How does this scripture apply to your role as a father?

Personal Reflection Space

What progress did I make yesterday towards my goals?

What is one thing I learned about myself yesterday?

What blessings did I notice yesterday?

Emotional Check-in

How do I feel today?

Why do I feel this way?

How do these emotions affect my parenting?

Daily Action Steps

What are today's primary goals and action plans I will take toward my SMART goals?

What actions will I take today that address the four core virtues of courage, fortitude, faith, and love?

Prayer Focus

What are my prayers for today to grow as a father?

What are my prayers for my children today?

What are my prayers for my marriage and family today?

What other prayers do I have today?

Day 24 – Daily Devotional and Journal

Today's Date:

Fathering Strong Daily Focus

Core Strength and Virtue: Marriage Relationships & Fortitude

Quote*: "A successful marriage requires falling in love many times, always with the same person." - Mignon McLaughlin*

Fatherhood Tip: Recommit to your marriage vows today. Share the moment with your children.

Today's Scripture Focus

"Love never fails." - 1 Corinthians 13:8

How does this scripture apply to your role as a father?

Personal Reflection Space

What progress did I make yesterday towards my goals?

What is one thing I learned about myself yesterday?

What blessings did I notice yesterday?

Emotional Check-in
How do I feel today?

Why do I feel this way?

How do these emotions affect my parenting?

Daily Action Steps
What are today's primary goals and action plans I will take toward my SMART goals?

What actions will I take today that address the four core virtues of courage, fortitude, faith, and love?

Prayer Focus
What are my prayers for today to grow as a father?

What are my prayers for my children today?

What are my prayers for my marriage and family today?

What other prayers do I have today?

Day 25– Daily Devotional and Journal

Today's Date:

Fathering Strong Daily Focus

Core Strength and Virtue: Father-Child Bonding & Love

Quote: *"A father's love is reflected in his child's eyes." – Unknown*

Fatherhood Tip: Create a new family tradition that expresses your love.

Today's Scripture Focus

"See what great love the Father has lavished on us." - 1 John 3:1

How does this scripture apply to your role as a father?

Personal Reflection Space

What progress did I make yesterday towards my goals?

What is one thing I learned about myself yesterday?

What blessings did I notice yesterday?

Emotional Check-in

How do I feel today?

Why do I feel this way?

How do these emotions affect my parenting?

Daily Action Steps

What are today's primary goals and action plans I will take toward my SMART goals?

What actions will I take today that address the four core virtues of courage, fortitude, faith, and love?

Prayer Focus

What are my prayers for today to grow as a father?

What are my prayers for my children today?

What are my prayers for my marriage and family today?

What other prayers do I have today?

Day 26 – Daily Devotional and Journal

Today's Date:

Fathering Strong Daily Focus

Core Strength and Virtue: Emotional Wealth & Faith

Quote: *"Faith is the art of holding on to things in spite of your changing moods and circumstances." - C.S. Lewis*

Fatherhood Tip: Practice emotional regulation through prayer and meditation with your children.

Today's Scripture Focus

"Cast all your anxiety on him because he cares for you." - 1 Peter 5:7

How does this scripture apply to your role as a father?

Personal Reflection Space

What progress did I make yesterday towards my goals?

What is one thing I learned about myself yesterday?

What blessings did I notice yesterday?

Emotional Check-in

How do I feel today?

Why do I feel this way?

How do these emotions affect my parenting?

Daily Action Steps

What are today's primary goals and action plans I will take toward my SMART goals?

What actions will I take today that address the four core virtues of courage, fortitude, faith, and love?

Prayer Focus

What are my prayers for today to grow as a father?

What are my prayers for my children today?

What are my prayers for my marriage and family today?

What other prayers do I have today?

Day 27 – Daily Devotional and Journal

Today's Date:

Fathering Strong Daily Focus

Core Strength and Virtue: Spiritual Health & Courage

Quote: *"Courage is fear that has said its prayers." - Dorothy Bernard*

Fatherhood Tip: Stand up for your beliefs today. Let your children see your conviction

Today's Scripture Focus

"Be on your guard; stand firm in the faith; be courageous; be strong." - 1 Corinthians 16:13

How does this scripture apply to your role as a father?

Personal Reflection Space

What progress did I make yesterday towards my goals?

What is one thing I learned about myself yesterday?

What blessings did I notice yesterday?

Emotional Check-in

How do I feel today?

Why do I feel this way?

How do these emotions affect my parenting?

Daily Action Steps

What are today's primary goals and action plans I will take toward my SMART goals?

What actions will I take today that address the four core virtues of courage, fortitude, faith, and love?

Prayer Focus

What are my prayers for today to grow as a father?

What are my prayers for my children today?

What are my prayers for my marriage and family today?

What other prayers do I have today?

Day 28 – Daily Devotional and Journal

Today's Date:

Fathering Strong Daily Focus

Core Strength and Virtue: Marriage Relationships & Fortitude

Quote: *"The greatest gift a father can give his children is to love their mother." - Theodore Hesburgh*

Fatherhood Tip: Plan a meaningful date night with your spouse. Strong marriages create secure children.

Today's Scripture Focus

"Love bears all things, believes all things, hopes all things, endures all things."
- 1 Corinthians 13:7

How does this scripture apply to your role as a father?

Personal Reflection Space

What progress did I make yesterday towards my goals?

What is one thing I learned about myself yesterday?

What blessings did I notice yesterday?

Emotional Check-in

How do I feel today?

Why do I feel this way?

How do these emotions affect my parenting?

Daily Action Steps

What are today's primary goals and action plans I will take toward my SMART goals?

What actions will I take today that address the four core virtues of courage, fortitude, faith, and love?

Prayer Focus

What are my prayers for today to grow as a father?

What are my prayers for my children today?

What are my prayers for my marriage and family today?

What other prayers do I have today?

Week 4 - Check-In Plan

Vision Statement Review

Do I feel this week's actions aligned with my vision statement? Why or why not?

What changes do I need to make to my vision statement?

Last Week Reflection

What wins can I celebrate?

What challenges did I face?

What Lessons did I learn?

This Week's SMART Goal Focus

SMART Goals	Why this goal matters	Actions I will take

Resource Management

What am I doing that I can delegate this week?

What can I simplify or reprioritize to provide more time to focus on my SMART goals?

What am I currently doing that I can eliminate?

Quality Time Planning With My Children

Child's Name   **Activity Planned**   **When Scheduled**

Family Connection Activities I Plan for This Week

Planned Family Activities   **When?**

What family spiritual focus activities do I plan for this week

Self-care & Growth

What activities will I do this week to continue to grow as a father?

What activities will I do this week to improve my health?

What activities will I do this week to improve my spiritual growth?

Weekly Prayer

What will be my prayer focus for this week?

Notes & Ideas

What additional thoughts, inspirations, or reminders should I document for this week?

Day 29 – Daily Devotional and Journal

Today's Date:

Fathering Strong Daily Focus

Core Strength and Virtue: Father-Child Bonding & Faith

Quote: *"A father's legacy is not measured in material wealth, but in the richness of character he instills in his children." – Unknown*

Fatherhood Tip: Share a story from your own faith journey with your children today. Your vulnerability creates a connection.

Today's Scripture Focus

But as for me and my house, we will serve the Lord." - Joshua 24:15

How does this scripture apply to your role as a father?

Personal Reflection Space

What progress did I make yesterday towards my goals?

What is one thing I learned about myself yesterday?

What blessings did I notice yesterday?

Emotional Check-in

How do I feel today?

Why do I feel this way?

How do these emotions affect my parenting?

Daily Action Steps

What are today's primary goals and action plans I will take toward my SMART goals?

What actions will I take today that address the four core virtues of courage, fortitude, faith, and love?

Prayer Focus

What are my prayers for today to grow as a father?

What are my prayers for my children today?

What are my prayers for my marriage and family today?

What other prayers do I have today?

Day 30 – Daily Devotional and Journal

Today's Date:

<u>Fathering Strong Daily Focus</u>

Core Strength and Virtue: Integration of All Virtues

Quote: *"The quality of a father can be seen in the goals, dreams, and aspirations he sets not only for himself but for his family." - Reed Markham*

Fatherhood Tip: Review your growth over these 30 days and set three specific goals for continuing your fatherhood journey.

<u>Today's Scripture Focus</u>

"Be strong and courageous. Do not be afraid; do not be discouraged, for the Lord your God will be with you wherever you go." - Joshua 1:9

How does this scripture apply to your role as a father?

<u>Personal Reflection Space</u>

What progress did I make yesterday towards my goals?

What is one thing I learned about myself yesterday?

What blessings did I notice yesterday?

Emotional Check-in

How do I feel today?

Why do I feel this way?

How do these emotions affect my parenting?

Daily Action Steps

What are today's primary goals and action plans I will take toward my SMART goals?

What actions will I take today that address the four core virtues of courage, fortitude, faith, and love?

Prayer Focus

What are my prayers for today to grow as a father?

What are my prayers for my children today?

What are my prayers for my marriage and family today?

What other prayers do I have today?

Notes

Beyond 30 Days: Continuing Your Fatherhood Journey

Completing this 30-day devotional marks not an ending but a significant milestone in your ongoing fatherhood journey. Over the past month, you've established foundational habits, gained valuable insights, and taken intentional steps toward becoming the father God designed you to be. The question now becomes: How do you maintain and build upon this momentum?

Celebrating Your Progress

Before looking ahead, take time to acknowledge how far you've come. Review your journal entries from Day 1 through Day 30, noting specific areas of growth and transformation. Perhaps you've developed greater patience with your children, improved your listening skills, or established more consistent family devotional times. These victories, both large and small, deserve recognition and celebration.

Consider writing a letter to yourself documenting the changes you've observed in your fatherhood approach and the impact these shifts have had on your family relationships. This reflection serves as encouragement and a powerful reminder of what's possible when you commit to intentional growth.

Refining Your Vision

With a month of focused reflection behind you, you now have the opportunity to revisit and refine your fatherhood vision statement. Your initial vision, while valuable, was created before this transformative journey. Now, with deeper insights and practical experience, you can sharpen and expand this guiding document.

Ask yourself: Has my understanding of my role as a father evolved? Have certain priorities shifted or clarified? What new aspirations have emerged that should be incorporated into my vision? This refined vision statement will serve as your North Star for the next phase of your fatherhood journey.

Establishing Sustainable Rhythms

The daily devotional structure has helped you establish a rhythm of reflection and intentional action. Now is the time to create a sustainable pattern that suits your unique life circumstances. While daily reflection remains ideal, the specific format may need adjustment to fit your long-term lifestyle.

Consider these approaches to maintaining momentum:

- ➢ Morning reflection sessions that combine Scripture reading, prayer, and brief journaling focused on the day ahead
- ➢ Evening review periods where you assess the day's fatherhood moments and set intentions for tomorrow
- ➢ Weekly deeper dives that allow for more extensive reflection and planning
- ➢ Monthly comprehensive reviews of your progress and challenges

The key is consistency rather than perfection. A brief daily connection with God focused on your fatherhood journey will prove more transformative than occasional lengthy sessions.

Deepening Your Core Strengths

The six core strengths explored in this devotional—physical health, spiritual health, emotional wealth, financial wealth, marriage relationships, and child connections—continue to serve as the foundation of strong fatherhood. Moving forward, consider focusing on one strength area each month for more concentrated growth.

For example, you might dedicate February to strengthening your marriage, March to financial stewardship, and April to emotional health. This focused approach allows for deeper exploration while maintaining awareness of how each area connects to your overall fatherhood effectiveness.

For each monthly focus, create specific SMART goals that build upon the insights gained during your 30-day journey. These goals should stretch you while remaining achievable within your current life season. You can continue to use the resources and devotional templates available on the fatheringstrongbook.com website to support your ongoing growth in each area.

Expanding Your Fatherhood Community

The journey ahead will be significantly enhanced through intentional connection with other fathers committed to growth. Consider these pathways to community:

- ➢ Form a Fathering Strong group that meets monthly to discuss challenges, share victories, and provide mutual encouragement. The Fathering Strong website offers resources for starting and facilitating such groups.

- ➢ Find a fatherhood mentor—someone further along in their journey who can provide wisdom and perspective based on experience. Their guidance can prove invaluable during challenging seasons.

- ➢ Become a mentor to a younger father, sharing the insights you've gained through this devotional and your ongoing growth. Teaching others reinforces your learning and multiplies your impact.

- ➢ Join the online Fathering Strong community through the app or website, where you'll find ongoing support, additional resources, and connections with fathers worldwide.

Remember that isolation diminishes your effectiveness while community amplifies your growth. The challenges of fatherhood were never meant to be navigated alone.

Continuing Your Learning Journey

Your growth as a father requires ongoing learning and exposure to new perspectives. Consider these pathways for continued development:

- ➢ Read one book on fatherhood, family relationships, or spiritual leadership each quarter. The Fathering Strong website offers many articles on fatherhood.

- ➢ Listen to the Fathering Strong podcast on fatherhood and family leadership during your commute or exercise time. These bite-sized learning opportunities can significantly impact your thinking over time.

- ➢ Attend a fatherhood conference or retreat annually. These immersive experiences provide concentrated learning and connection opportunities that can catalyze significant growth.

Implementing Seasonal Reviews

While weekly check-ins help maintain momentum, quarterly and annual reviews provide deeper reflection and course correction opportunities. Schedule these more comprehensive assessments at regular intervals:

> ➤ **Quarterly reviews** (every three months) to evaluate progress on your goals, identify emerging challenges and adjust your approach as needed

> ➤ **Annual retreats**—ideally an entire day set aside—to comprehensively assess your fatherhood journey, celebrate growth, process disappointments, and establish direction for the year ahead

These structured review periods help prevent drift and ensure your fatherhood remains intentional rather than reactive. Many fathers find it valuable to include their spouse in these reviews, gaining their perspective and strengthening alignment in parenting approaches.

Embracing Seasons and Transitions

Your fatherhood journey will naturally evolve as your children grow and family circumstances change. Each stage brings unique challenges and opportunities that require adaptation and new learning:

> ➤ The hands-on parenting of young children gradually shifts to the guiding and coaching of adolescents

> ➤ The active direction of teenagers eventually transforms into the supportive encouragement of young adult children

> ➤ The daily presence of children living at home changes to an intentional connection with adult children, building their own lives

Rather than resisting these transitions, embrace them as opportunities for growth. Each new season invites you to develop different aspects of your fatherhood and discover new dimensions of being a Godly father.

Recommitting to the Four Virtues

The four virtues that have guided your journey—courage, fortitude, faith, and love—remain essential as you move forward. Regularly revisit these foundational qualities, asking yourself:

> ➤ **Courage:** Where am I playing it safe rather than leading with boldness? What difficult conversations or decisions am I avoiding?

> ➤ **Fortitude:** How am I maintaining consistency in my fatherhood commitments? Where do I need greater perseverance?

- ➢ **Faith**: Am I trusting God's guidance in my parenting decisions? How am I modeling dependence on God for my children?

- ➢ **Love:** Are my actions consistently communicating unconditional love? How can I more effectively demonstrate love to each family member in their unique love language?

When consistently cultivated, these virtues transform not just your actions but your very character as a father. They become the internal compass that guides your decisions and responses in every situation.

Creating Your Legacy Plan

With the foundation established through this devotional, you're now positioned to think more intentionally about your long-term fatherhood legacy. Consider creating a written legacy plan that addresses the following:

- ➢ Values and principles you want to instill in your children and grandchildren

- ➢ Faith traditions and practices you wish to establish or maintain across generations

- ➢ Financial wisdom and resources you intend to pass down

- ➢ Life lessons and stories you want to preserve and share

- ➢ Skills and knowledge you hope to transfer to the next generation

This legacy planning transforms your day-to-day fathering from isolated actions into a coherent narrative that spans generations. It connects your current efforts to outcomes that may unfold decades into the future.

The Journey Continues

As you close this 30-day devotional and open the next chapter of your fatherhood journey, remember that growth is rarely linear. You'll experience seasons of significant progress and periods that feel like plateaus or even setbacks. Throughout these variations, maintain your commitment to the process, trusting that God is faithfully working in and through you.

The father you're becoming is exactly the father your children need. Each step of intentional growth, each moment of humble learning, and each instance of choosing love over convenience shapes not just your fatherhood but your children's future. Your investment in becoming a stronger father creates returns that extend far beyond what you can currently imagine.

Continue forward with confidence, knowing that the God who called you to fatherhood walks alongside you, providing wisdom, strength, and grace for each new challenge. Your journey to stronger fatherhood has just begun, and its impact will echo through generations.

"May the God of hope fill you with all joy and peace as you trust in him, so that you may overflow with hope by the power of the Holy Spirit." (Romans 15:13)

Fatherhood Prayer

Heavenly Father,
As I complete this 30-day journey of growth and reflection, I come before You with a grateful heart. Thank You for walking beside me each step, strengthening me when I felt weak, and showing me what it truly means to father with courage, fortitude, faith, and love.

Lord, I acknowledge that every good gift comes from You, including the sacred privilege of being a father. Thank You for entrusting me with Your precious children and showing me, through Your perfect example, how to lead them with strength and tenderness.

I ask for Your continued guidance as I strive to be the father You've called me to be. Help me remain steadfast in my commitment to spiritual growth, knowing that my children learn more from my example than my words. Give me the wisdom to make decisions that honor You and serve my family's highest good.

Grant me the physical strength to be present and engaged in my children's lives, the emotional wisdom to connect with their hearts, and the spiritual discernment to guide them toward Your truth. Help me create an atmosphere of stability and security in our home, where Your love flows freely, and Your presence is honored.

Father, I pray for the fortitude to maintain the healthy patterns I've established during these past thirty days. When challenges arise, remind me to put on Your full armor, standing firm in faith as I protect and provide for those You've placed in my care. Help me balance work and family life with wisdom, managing our resources in ways that honor You and secure my family's future.

Deepen my connection with my spouse, Lord, strengthening our partnership as we raise our children in Your ways. Help me model for my children what it means to love sacrificially and lead humbly. When I fall short, give me the courage to ask for forgiveness and the grace to begin again.

Thank You for the brotherhood of other fathers who share this journey. Continue to surround me with men who will encourage my growth, challenge my thinking, and point me toward Your truth. Help me be that same source of support and wisdom for others.

As I look ahead, I ask for Your help in remaining intentional about my growth as a father. Keep my goals aligned with Your purposes, my heart attuned to Your voice, and my actions consistent with Your Word. Help me leave a legacy of faithful fatherhood that will impact future generations.

Most of all, thank You for being my perfect Heavenly Father, loving me unconditionally, and showing me what true strength looks like through Your Son, Jesus Christ. May everything I do as a father bring honor to Your name and draw my family closer to Your heart. In Jesus' name, Amen.

About the Author

Bruce Stapleton authored *"Fathering Strong - God's Blueprint for Leading Your Family,"* a comprehensive blueprint accompanying this 30-day devotional and journal. He combines corporate leadership experience, entrepreneurial success, and deep spiritual commitment in his work on Biblical fatherhood.

Bruce's expertise stems from 25+ years creating and teaching Christian parenting education through Urban Light Ministries, where he leads the Fathering Strong program and previously served as Board Chairman. He helped develop the Fathering Strong app and podcast, providing daily Bible-based inspiration to fathers while managing the ministry's digital presence, establishing himself as a voice in faith-based fatherhood education.

Bruce's background includes executive positions at NCR Corporation, leading worldwide services marketing and strategic planning. His entrepreneurial spirit created the award-winning Lifegevity program in preventive health, demonstrating his talent for practical solutions. As a college digital marketing instructor with a Business and Economics degree and MBA, he brings academic knowledge and real-world experience to his teachings.

Bruce's perspective is shaped by fathering four children, being grandfather to four, and appreciating positive male role models across generations. His father and grandfather taught him woodworking and outdoor activities, informing his understanding of building lasting connections with children. His 42-year marriage and church ministry involvement strengthen his authority in teaching Biblical fatherhood principles.

Through his writing, Bruce delivers inspiration and practical tools fathers need to impact their children's lives and communities. He is the creator of the Fatherhood Awakening process and fatherhood evaluation, bridging Biblical teachings and modern parenting challenges to offer a clear path to building stronger, faith-centered families.

For more information, visit his LinkedIn profile at www.linkedin.com/in/bruce-stapleton.

Notes

For more resources go to:

www.fatheringstrongbook.com

Purchase the book that accompanies this devotional

Fathering Strong – God's Blueprint for Leading Your Family

Purchase online at all major book outlets.

12-week Workshop for Churches

Interested in using this devotional in a fatherhood class? Participant Workbooks and Facilitator Guides are available. Contact information@fatheringstrongbook.com for bundle discounts.

Join a fatherhood community where you can connect with other fathers, get support and encouragement throughout your fatherhood journey, and become empowered to be the best dad you can be. Join this free community today!

Join at www.fatheringstrong.com

www.ingramcontent.com/pod-product-compliance
Lightning Source LLC
Chambersburg PA
CBHW081659120626
46550CB00010B/2955